Playbook Wins...

"Every game that is played in the world has a playbook for it. Jim has perfected the playbook for men who play in this game as husband and leader. As you incorporate the tactics from this playbook, you'll score every time. If you want to survive in this game of marriage and win, here's the way to do it. Read this!"

Bishop George Searight
Founder and Senior Pastor of the
Abundant Life Family Worship Church, New Brunswick, NJ

"Just imagine, if you had traveled to another planet and the aliens that you encountered received you and gave you an audience. There are two things that you would need to be effective in this situation. First, you will need to have important information to communicate and second you will need to speak their language. Sometimes it seems like the world that we live in has gotten so far from God's original intent for men, marriage and family that earth seems like a strange planet in a distant galaxy. Well, I've got good news, Pastor Jim Hart has an important message and he has communicated that message in a language that most men speak. Jim has painted an instructional masterpiece on the canvas of sports terminology, concepts and analogies. His message is clear and concise, true and biblically based, and finally tried and proven. Do yourself and your family a favor and read this enlightening work on *The Great Husband's Playbook*, before you fall too far behind and your time expires. I'm sure you will find several plays that will bring you a desired outcome and a strategy that can lead you to victory."

Bishop Eric K. Clark of Cleveland, OH

"Jewish tradition teaches that scripture speaks 'best through the language of ordinary people.'" Through his engaging use of sports language, my colleague Pastor Jim inspires husbands to think about how we can all build stronger marriages and families in an accessible language we can all understand."

Rabbi Dan Dorsch, Temple Beth Shalom, Livingston, NJ.

"Every man should read this book before getting married, if possible, because it will help you stay married. If you are married, don't read it unless you are ready to change and make *plays*."

Vaughn L. McKoy, JD,MBA
President and CEO, The McKoy Group, LLC and Author of
Playing Up: One Man's Rise from Public Housing to Public
Service through Mentorship

"The language and culture of pro sports in America speaks to millions of men and women every day. *The Great Husband's Playbook*, an awesome and practical application of those ideas and procedures to one of the oldest and most important institutions known to mankind. It's one of the keys to being the difference maker, the M.V.P. of "Team Family".

Bill Daughtry
98.7 ESPN Radio, New York

"As a veteran NFL coach and husband, I learned several strategies to winning with my life that I wish I could have learned 22 years ago. Being a great husband requires deliberate action and commitment to your wife and family for a championship caliber lifestyle. *The Great Husband's Playbook*, is a must read for married couples who desire stronger, happy, marriages.

Thomas McGaughey Jr.
2007 Super Bowl Champion
Special Teams Coordinator - SF 49ers

"Pastor Jim Hart is cleverly instructive as coach and teacher in *The Great Husband's Playbook: Winning Plays for a Victorious Marriage*. His book is artful, creative, and sensitive. It invites us to "divorce and dispel" the selfish conviction that we as husbands, alone, rule; and "marry" into the belief that a successful marriage is an achievable higher calling that requires consistent companionship."

Anthony P. Carter
Global Diversity and Social Justice
Writer and Lecturer

"In Business, the book "Good to Great" by Jim Collins has been a must read for all business people, in family life, *The Great Husband's Playbook: Winning Plays for a Victorious Marriage* by Pastor Jim, is the must read book for every husband."

Peter M. Crowley
President & CEO
Princeton Regional Chamber of Commerce

"Jim's *Great Husband's Playbook*, is a strategic compilation of the most effective plays for men to review and study as they strive to become great husbands. He tackles all of the daily distractions that can become hindrances to husbands if they are not on the same team with their wives. Leading our wives and families to continuous victories above 500 is all that really matters in the game of life."

E. Earl Jenkins
CEO, The Jenkins Group

"Great" is an important goal to strive for, whether it's in sports, politics, business or marriage. Pastor Jim is right to urge everyone to be the best they can be, especially in their relationships with loved ones. Congratulations to Pastor Jim on this insightful read full of strong, real-life advice."

Mayor James Cahill

"Marriage is serious business, but it can also be fun. After more than 50 years with my bride, I can vouch for the wisdom Pastor Hart has presented in this wonderful work. If you're a new husband, this book can keep you ahead of the game. If you've got some years behind you, *The Great Husband's Playbook* can breathe new life into your "second half."

Solomon Hicks
Founder/CEO, Hicks Global Enterprises

"I already thought that I was a great husband, but through each chapter, verse and quote in this book, Pastor Hart illustrates in many ways how even the great husbands can step up their game and take your marriage to the next level. Great husbands make happy wives... Happy wives make great marriages. "

Judge Carl L. Marshall, J.M.C.

"This is *Good to Great* for Husbands! You can't be a great husband without figuring out the right plays to run on the field of marriage. Pastor Jim has given each of us tools to make a difference in Team Family!"

Dr. Jeffrey Robinson
Associate Professor, Rutgers Business School
International Speaker and Author

"A husband's role in leading his family is one of the most important responsibilities bestowed upon him in the marital covenant. *The Great Husband's Playbook*, provides men with clear winning strategies and common marriage scenarios to help good husbands become great. Greatness requires practice, diligence, confidence, and a fearless mindset that your efforts will lead to success. Jim's Playbook is a timeless gift to men seeking to win at life's daily challenges in leading their wives and families."

Dr. Alex O. Ellis
Tied To Greatness

"I may not know a lot about football, but I do know what a win is... especially in marriage. The plays in Jim's book give great principles that will help you go from good to GREAT in the game of marriage. As a wife of forty years, I can validate the strategies from this playbook will guarantee a win with your wife. The insights in this playbook will help you score big in your role as husband and father. If you want your marriage to reach Super Bowl status, this book is a must read!"

Pastor Mary Searight
Abundant Life Family Worship Church, New Brunswick, NJ

"Jim has written a practical book that will save or strengthen your marriage. He understands the great responsibility it takes to be a godly man and the great rewards that come when you build your life and marriage on the Word of God. I highly recommend *The Great Husband's Playbook*. With this book, you can finally experience the championship marriage you have been destined to have."

Pastor John Edmondson, Victory in Christ Christian Center
Westville, NJ and Certified Christian Counselor, NCCA

"Jim has drawn up several game winning plays for every husband to execute to become great. He skillfully uses sports analogies to tackle some hard-hitting marital issues, while offering practical coaching tips to successfully address them. This is a must read for every husband who refuses to be a spectator and wants to be a game-changer for his family. *The Great Husband's Playbook* is a rallying cry for men to push themselves harder to win in an arena where it really counts. Use this Playbook as a guide and become a hall of fame husband, father and leader.

Leo L. Sherard
Senior Pastor, Light of the World Family Worship Church

"We can't conquer what we won't confront and we can't confront what we don't identify. I love how this book shows men in a way they can understand (through sports) how to identify in own their lives and marriages the areas that could be sabotaging them from being all they are called to be. As the bible says in Amos 3:3... we perish due to lack of knowledge; Well Jim gives us in his book both practical and spiritual knowledge from his own marriage, years of study and counseling, to help our own marriages so they can be all they were designed to be. This book is a must read for every man or husband in your life!"

Pastor Isha Edmondson, Co-Pastor Victory in Christ Christian Center, Westville, NJ and Certified Christian Counselor, NCCA

"I think Coach Jim is on to something that today's husbands can relate to when it comes to marriage and families. His thought provocative comparisons of sports and marriage are really spelled out in his playbook with the detailed X's & O's of a game plan to be a winner in the most important game of all... Marriage!"

Lt. Jack Doyle

THE GREAT HUSBAND'S PLAYBOOK

Winning Plays for a Victorious Marriage

By Jim Hart MSW, LSW

Foreword by Chris Broussard
NBA Analyst and Reporter

Scripture quotations are from The Holy Bible, New International Version® Copyright ©1973, 1978, 1984 by the International Bible Society.

Printed in the United States of America

2016 First Edition

10 9 8 7 6 5 4 3 2 1

Subject Index:
Hart, Jim
Title: The Great Husband's Playbook: Winning Plays for a Victorious Marriage
1. Marriage 2. Family 3. Christian 4. Inspirational 5. Self-Help
Paperback ISBN: 978-0-578-17691-8

The Hart Company

thegreathusbandsplaybook.com

DEDICATION

This book is dedicated to the most important people in my life, my wife Yetunde, and our three sons Samuel, Daniel, and Gabriel.

Yetunde, I truly thank you for your love, patience, faithfulness, and grace. I am without a doubt a better man and *great* husband because of you. I love you with all of my heart and I am grateful you said "Yes" to marrying me all those years ago. I could not and would not have written this book without your full support so thank you for your blessing to complete this project. Thank you for also supporting and encouraging my practice with married couples over the years. Your sacrifices will never be missed or forgotten and will most certainly be rewarded. Love you always…

Samuel, Daniel, and Gabriel…I thank you for loving me unconditionally. Raising you guys has taught me so much about life, love, and relationships. One of the main reasons I wrote this book was so that you would one day have a Playbook to follow to be a *great* husband to your future wives. Your love and support is more than a father deserves and more than I have earned. Love you always...

ACKNOWLEDGEMENTS

There are so many people to thank for helping me complete this book. To my biological father, James S. Hart II, I thank you for your honesty, perseverance, commitment, and fidelity in your own relationships, it has been inspiring and encouraging. Thank you for always loving and supporting me in all of my endeavors. To my Mother, Gloria Hyde, I want to thank you for your support, for listening to my ideas and giving me feedback throughout the process. To my step-father, Calvin Hyde, I thank you for showing me how to blend two families together. Watching you love my Mom has been a great example to follow. Your love and support has been amazing. To my Pastors, Bishop George and Pastor Mary Searight, I thank you for welcoming me into the church and your family as a son. Thank you for entrusting me with the task of counseling couples within and outside of the church. Those opportunities planted the seeds which have manifested into this project.

To my editor, Kim Rouse, I thank you for your support, encouragement and *patience* throughout this process. Your ability to take an author's unpolished concepts and turn them into gold is amazing. To Chris Broussard, thank you for believing in the project, for your support and for writing the Foreword. To all the couples I've ever had the privilege counseling, thank you for allowing me to enter into your world and entrusting me with your deepest pains, secrets, arguments, and disagreements, and believing I had the answer to your problems. All of you have certainly taught me more about marriage and love than I'll ever teach you.

Contents

Contents

FOREWORD

What man wouldn't want to be an All-Star? Whether a lawyer, engineer, school teacher or athlete - whatever the career - we all want to be successful. We all want to be the best. But why don't we apply that same competitive drive to marriage? Why don't we make it a priority to become an All-Star husband? In *The Great Husband's Playbook: Winning Plays for a Victorious Marriage*, Jim Hart challenges us to do just that. In fact, he does more than challenge. He provides a step-by-step blueprint for becoming an elite husband.

Like many men, Jim is an avid sports fan. Like many men, he would have loved to have become a top-flight athlete. But like most of us, he lacked the talent to make it to the pros. But Jim found something else he could be a Michael Jordan at: marriage. In a unique approach that makes all the sense in the world, he takes the terms, teachings and examples of sports and applies them to marriage. As it turns out, being a great quarterback and a great husband require many of the same qualities and traits. An effective team captain and a trusted family leader have much in common. You'll find out what in *The Great Husband's Playbook*.

In a style that's straightforward and blunt (much like that of a good coach), Jim tells you what plays work and what plays don't. He tells you how to read your wife and offers practical advice about every aspect of the marital relationship. You'll learn how a blue-chip husband handles himself at work, during a disagreement, in financial matters, around other women, even in the bedroom. Teaching like this is invaluable, especially in today's America, where fatherlessness and divorce are rampant. So many boys grow up without fathers to show them the character, responsibilities and joys of a great husband. Jim fills that void with knowledge that is timely, tested, and of the utmost importance.

I have been married for 20 years, my parents have been married for 50 years, and both sets of my grandparents were married for more than half a century, so I know what it takes to make marriage work. Yet I still learned plenty from *The Great Husband's Playbook.* During every chapter, I found myself saying, "I never thought of it that way." I trust that you will have the same experience. And I trust that you - and perhaps more importantly, your wife - will be as appreciative as I am that Jim shared his playbook.

Chris Broussard
NBA Analyst and Reporter
President of The K.I.N.G. Movement

INTRODUCTION

Step Up Your Game

Men, as the leader of your family, now is the time to make a commitment to be a *great* husband to your wife. Achieving greatness is difficult. It takes deliberate action, sacrifice, planning and steadfast focus. Greatness is often used to refer to individual athletes or sports teams. I love sports, in fact, football, basketball, baseball, soccer, hockey, golf, and tennis, all garner my attention at some point throughout the seasons. Football, is by far my favorite, and many of the analogies and strategies contained in this Playbook relate to football, yet all team sports are reflected throughout to demonstrate important marital points and keys to winning with your wife.

Sports are one of the most universal male experiences and passions. That's why I believe this sports theme will help men understand and apply the applicable concepts in this book to their marriage. My goal in compiling this Playbook was to use the wisdom of previous generations along with a current understanding of the dynamics of today's marital relationships to produce simple plays and strategies that husbands can follow to be *great*. All of the plays are practical, realistic and doable. Of course, these are not the end all strategies, but if you make a conscious effort to work through them, your marriage will be significantly enhanced.

These strategies were created from four different sources: (i) those that I've decided to live by as my wife and I grow old together; (ii) some were discovered only after I failed to run the play correctly, or not at all, and experienced the penalties for not doing so; (iii) others are from the hundreds of married couples that I've counseled and witnessed husbands ignoring or fumbling critical plays that were important to their wives; and finally (iv) plays that I picked up from men in my inner circle who continuously help to shape me into being the *great* husband that God designed.

Throughout this book, you will also find sports language, quotes, and situations to help illustrate the skill sets needed to become a *great* husband. This Playbook is broken down based on plays for your life from a personal, professional, financial, and spiritual angle. All four of these areas directly affect our roles as husbands. Of course, there may be plays that don't apply to your specific marital situation, as no book will completely capture everyone's experiences. However, like any good leader, stick with the plays that work for you, and set aside those that don't resonate in your marriage.

There are lots of average husbands in the world today, but my hope is to increase the number of *great* husbands, which we don't have enough of. I believe that one of the primary reasons for the lack of *great* husbands is the breakdown of the traditional nuclear family. Consequently, many men lacked the role models in their home to give them a first-hand look at what being a man actually looked like, let alone the requirements for being a *great* husband. Schools, churches and other social institutions are trying to provide this information, but getting men to attend and follow through with implementation is a continuous challenge. Furthermore, the plays that today's husbands can use to be *great* in many respects have changed. Those changes transcend race, religion, and socioeconomic status. At the same time, there are plays that all *great* husbands have followed for decades that still work today.

Every championship sports team has a great leader. Whether it be the head coach, the quarterback in football, or the team captain in other sports, great leaders steer their teams to victory, and make everyone on the team better. In order to be a *great* husband, you must take on the characteristics of great leaders to lead the most important team in your life, *Team Family-* your wife and children. Leadership is never easy, and you often face the highs and lows of doing good and failing miserably. However, your strategy in bouncing back after defeat is the key to continuous success. As a husband, be prepared to lead in any capacity that is necessary to move your family forward. If you try to master this entire Playbook in a few days, you will probably become discouraged, frustrated, and quit. This is a lifetime commitment towards becoming *great*.

Keep in mind, that there isn't a *Number One* play to greatness. The truth is, your *Number One* play is probably the one that is most important to your wife at this present moment.

Over time, as your marriage grows and her needs change, so will the *Number One* play for you. Be sure to walk through these plays with your wife to discover which ones can strengthen your marriage. As a pastor, this Playbook also has Biblical references because I believe having a relationship with God is the blueprint for a successful marriage. Pray and listen to His voice for direction.

Finally, I offer this two-minute warning piece of advice: In marriage, your season is never over. Each day you should be in better shape, position, and mindset, than the day before, as you prepare to deal with life's challenges. You were drafted as a rookie husband with the hope of living up to your potential to lead *Team Family* to continuous victory. May this Playbook challenge, motivate, encourage and inspire you to stay above 500 as you take on the greatest role you'll ever have on this Earth—being a husband.

FIRST
QUARTER

CHAPTER 1

TEAM FAMILY

"If you aren't going all the way, why go at all?"

- Joe Namath

No matter what sports teams you played for and how great your team was, it will never compare to your role or success with *Team Family*. The success of your marriage will be directly determined by your leadership abilities, rather than your individual talent. In *The 21 Irrefutable Laws of Leadership*, John Maxwell points out that everything rises and falls on leadership. If you want a great marriage and a great relationship with your wife, you must be a *great* leader.

Husbands are called to lead *Team Family*. As the head of your wife, she is encouraged to follow your lead in everything. [1] Leadership means working hard on yourself and ensuring that you are the very best you can be in every area of your life. As the team captain, you must work to make all members of *Team*

Family the very best they can possibly be, given their talent, potential, and skill sets. You are to keep the team focused on small and large goals. It means sacrificing personal success to ensure there is team success. It means keeping the morale high when difficulties emerge and rallying the team when losses have been experienced. Equally important, is knowing how to handle success when it is earned.

Your wife is your teammate—your go-to person. If your team sport is basketball, you are the Center or Power Forward, and she is the Point Guard or Shooting Guard. Both positions are critical to the success of any championship contending team. Your wife needs you to lead the team and she will follow. She wants to trust that you will make the right decisions and that you have *Team Family's* best interests at heart.

No matter what sports team you played for, nor how great that team was, it will never compare to the team that you're now on with your wife. Our marriages need the characteristics that championship teams achieve for long-term success.

Check the Scoreboard

Our role as a husband is to love, care for, and protect our wife while nurturing her potential to our fullest ability. Starting today, try out a few practical plays to immediately get on the scoreboard with your wife as you work for *Team Family* to be a great husband:

1. *Sacrifice:* Be the first to sacrifice and the last to be rewarded. Your marriage will be filled with frustration and difficulty if you always want to be the first one

rewarded, and the last to sacrifice. This doesn't mean that you are never rewarded, it just means that your focus shifts from seeking rewards to scouting out times to sacrifice, so that your wife feels valued.

2. *Love Unconditionally*: Always unconditionally show love to your wife. Regardless of her past behaviors, your love must remain unconditional. That doesn't mean you become a doormat for dysfunctional or abusive behavior. It does mean, that you rise above your hurt and disappointment to love anyway.

3. *Profess Love*: Regularly tell your wife that you love her, you appreciate all she does for the family and how her beauty grows with each passing day. This three-cord approach will strengthen her self-esteem, increase her sense of significance, and calm any anxiety she may have that you'll look elsewhere for connection and intimacy.

4. *Reconnect:* When you come home from work, make a deliberate effort to reconnect with your wife *before* you reconnect with your children. Research shows that this is one of the most important times in the life of a marriage. Reconnect by giving her a "5 minute" hug. It's not that you literally hug for 5 minutes, but stay on the field long enough to release the stress from the day, until you both feel a genuine reconnection take place.

5. *Record:* Purchase a journal to begin recording every day at least one thing that you value and appreciate about your wife. At the end of the year, give her the journal as a gift of love. The writing and reflection process will

transform you more than you can imagine, because your thoughts are not focused on the negative, but the positive aspects of what you value and appreciate about her.

6. *Grace:* Show grace to your wife when she fails to meet your needs. Don't allow negative feelings to fester in your heart, which creates separation. Continually work on reconnection.

Extra Point:

7. *Giving:* Know your wife's shoe, dress, suit, and lingerie size, so that when you're out shopping you can surprise her with a gift. If your wife's love language is gifts, this will certainly fill her love tank!

CHAPTER 2

GREATNESS AND YOU

"I am the greatest. I said that even before I knew I was."
- **Muhammad Ali**

M en in America are obsessed with greatness. They love to identify, categorize, and classify greatness. Don't believe me? Turn on any sports talk radio show and inevitably you'll hear the host debate callers about: Who is the greatest quarterback to ever play in the NFL? Who is the greatest basketball player to ever play in the NBA? Which baseball team is the greatest to ever play in the Major Leagues? Wherever you find a group of men discussing a subject, the issues of defining, identifying, recognizing, and appreciating greatness, are bound to come up. Jim Collins' book, *Good to Great*, makes a compelling argument that good is the enemy of great. Collins tells us that very few people seek *great* lives because settling for the good life is a lot easier. Greatness is a difficult feat to accomplish, but with intentional action, diligence, and a clear strategy, success is bound to occur.

For instance, imagine if I told you that I had the formula to make you a great golfer would you follow it? If you play golf, the answer would be a resounding "Yes!" What if I told you that I had fool-proof strategies to make you a great business-man in thirty days, would you apply those strategies? If you are in business or want to start one, I'm sure the answer would be "Yes!" If I told you I had the plays to make you a great lover in bed, would you listen and apply the advice? This is an easy one, since most men love sex, the answer would definitely be "Yes!" Regardless of which topic I put before you, if you have an interest in it, you will choose being *great* over good each and every time. Especially, if you're given the right strategies with the belief that you can achieve it. Therefore, greatness is relative, because if you are interested in a topic, you will pursue it with passion.

Still, let's not overlook the fact that there are some great players who often settle for being average leaders. Average leadership hinders the great player just like it does husbands from the refinement and stretching needed to become *great.* Average will lead to complacency, and it won't produce the best possible expression of ourselves, to our wives, and our marital relationship. Husbands who settle for being average may also create a sense of unfulfillment in themselves and their wives. More often than not, such marriage discord isn't felt until years later, and the regret of lost opportunities becomes a hard reality to accept. Such regrets and the lingering questions of what I could have or should have achieved, will tug at your hearts for a long time.

Some will say that not everyone becomes *great* and not everyone can be *great* in their specific areas of interest. I beg to differ, because if you *desire* to be *great*, then that's the first necessary element for success. A second necessary factor is perspective. You may never become the greatest golfer like Tiger Woods or Rory McElroy, but you can become the greatest golfer that *you* can personally be. Yet, by maximizing your golf potential, you can achieve personal greatness, even if you never make the PGA Tour.

How does this apply to your role as a husband? If you have the motivation and desire to be a *great* husband, that goal is well within your reach. Regardless of how you've performed thus far, or how deficient you may be in certain areas, I truly believe greatness is within your reach. One factor often missing in how we define greatness is the idea of being a servant. We see this concept of servant leadership throughout the Bible. Jesus said if want to be great you have to be a servant. [2]. If you want to be first, you must be last.[3] The Apostle Paul, told men to love their wife as Christ loved the church. Jesus loved the church, so he demonstrated leadership by training and teaching the disciples to carry His message throughout the world. Then, He demonstrated servanthood by dying on the cross for the church, and willfully put his needs as secondary. As husbands, we are called to fulfill this same kind of servant leadership.

Great husbands are willing to serve their wives and help her fulfill her greatest potential. It is not a sign of weakness, nor does it diminish your masculinity. It takes maturity, responsibility, planning, and thoughtfulness to serve your wife as in the Bible. In serving her, as Christ loved the church, you help her achieve wholeness in every area of her life, and you serve out of your love for her. This isn't an easy thing to do. In fact, it is probably the toughest role you will ever have. Yet the toughest challenges earn the largest trophies for success.

Being a servant is difficult because it means seeking to fulfill, rather than being fulfilled. It means conquering your pride and ego, selfishness and laziness. However, the rewards for those who achieve greatness as a husband are life-changing. Your wife will love you more, respect you more, satisfy your sexual needs more, and be more eager to help you fulfill your potential. Serving, will in turn, transform your own life into having "more."

To further illustrate this servant-leadership perspective, there is a definition for a husband that has a British origin which describes a husband as a steward of the household. This may be a bit surprising to most Americans, but if you understand the role and responsibility of a husband the concept of a steward is an accurate description. Husbands are the ones primarily responsible for ensuring that their household is taken care of properly. This encompasses all aspects and relationships of their life. A wife has a significant influence in how the "household" is run, but the first and final level of responsibility rests on the husband's shoulders.

Furthermore, as a manager or steward, husbands must realize all that encompasses their "household" is on loan to them.

Husbands will need to give an account of how they managed their household on this Earth with their wife, children, family, and friends. The accounting will also take place in eternity when the husband leaves this Earth to be reunited with God.

You may not be a husband like someone else is to his wife, but that's not important. Unlike other areas in life that require us to prove and convince others that we're great, the only one you need to hear say, *"Sweetheart, you're a great husband,"* is your wife. Every day should be game day, and winning with your wife is all that really counts.

Your Leadership Matters

> *"...in any group of activity-whether in business, sports, or family-there has to be leadership or it won't be successful."*
>
> - **John Wooden**

Every athlete must go through a training and development period to refine his athletic skills, but also to maximize his leadership capacity. Often times the head coach is purposely preparing the star athlete to be the leader of the team. In the beginning of humanity, God took Adam on a similar preparation journey before Eve came on the scene. Adam learned to have a relationship with God. He was charged with tending to the Garden which developed his work ethic. He was given the responsibility of naming all the animals to ensure he was an effective communicator.

Adam had to realize that he could not live alone, he needed

others to be on his team. It was only at this moment that God then created Eve, because Adam was ready to lead. Adam is leading his wife in The Garden of Eden and they are a couple for a period of time enjoying the fruits of their labor. Like every other marital relationship, difficulty rears its ugly head. Unfortunately, Adam failed the leadership tests that came to Eve by the serpent from eating from the Tree of the Knowledge of Good and Evil[4].

Although that failure removed Adam and Eve from God's presence, it did not sever the relationship with God and one another. The failure made life more difficult, but it did not remove Adam from his responsibility to lead, love and cherish Eve. Despite our failures God still wants to have a relationship with us and our wives still want us to be the leader. You don't know how great of a leader you are when you have only experienced success, but you find the depths of your leadership capacity in the midst of failure.

Chasing Perfection

Before we move onto the other chapters, allow me to dispel the perfection myth. Perfection isn't real. It's like fantasy football when you've assembled the perfect quarterback to lead your perfect team. By now you're thinking, *Jim wants me to be perfect.* That's not where I'm going. The challenge for us as husbands is to be *great*, not perfect. Perfection will always elude us, no matter how hard we try to obtain it. Neither you nor your wife are perfect, so neither of you will be able to provide perfection on any relational level. Therefore, always keep in mind that greatness is our goal, not perfection.

Consider the next few analogies to further illustrate my point. Tom Brady is a great quarterback, but he hasn't won every playoff game. Tiger Woods is a great golfer, yet he has missed the cut in many tournaments. Roy Halladay is a Cy Young Award pitcher, but he never won a World Series. Pat Riley is a great basketball coach, yet many of his teams did not win championships. Warren Buffett is a great investor, but every stock he picks is not always profitable.

By now, the point should be clear, we will all make mistakes and fall short of our ambitions, goals, and success. Even though this is true for all of us, it doesn't disqualify us from being *great*. In fact, failure is a prerequisite for greatness.

"You can't win unless you learn how to lose."
- Kareem Abdul-Jabbar

Don't allow your past or present failures as a husband to cripple you from pursuing greatness. The nagging voices of your failures and mistakes will always whisper to your souls, but you don't have to listen to them. Try not to let guilt and shame of your past or present actions cause you to be discouraged, and therefore unwilling to achieve greatness as a husband. Even as I write this, there are past actions and decisions that I regret, which I can't do anything about now. The truth of the matter is, there are areas as a husband that I need to still improve upon and put in continuous work. I am not a perfect husband, but I am working every day toward greatness. Like me, the majority of husbands out there are a work in progress. Let's go ahead and start moving the chains. Remember the words from Nido Qubein, "Your present circumstances don't determine where you go; they merely determine where you start." As the quarterback husband-leader, for *Team Family*, learn to view your mistakes as a refining process to help advance those areas where you are lacking.

Achieving Greatness

The great teams that we've witnessed win championships recently all had similar characteristics: i) a desire to win, ii) great chemistry, iii) great talent, iv) a willingness to sacrifice and work hard, v) great coaching and vi) great role players. These teams would have never reached the pinnacle of championship success without great leadership. In fact, I would be hard pressed to name a team that won a title, but didn't have great leadership. Of course, I must mention Michael Jordan and the Chicago Bulls under Phil Jackson's leadership, as well as Kobe Bryant's leadership success with Phil Jackson at the helm. If we look at the 2012 & 2013 Miami Heat, they had LeBron James. The 2014 San Antonio Spurs had Tim Duncan and Greg Popovich. The 2013 Boston Red Sox had David Ortiz. The 2012 Baltimore Ravens had Ray Lewis. The 2009 New York Yankees had Derek Jeter. Each of these great players were great leaders. They performed when it mattered the most, and more importantly, made their teammates around them better.

Unfortunately, we could name several great players in every sport throughout history that had tremendous talent but either fell short of leadership excellence or failed miserably in the area of leadership. I won't mention names, but think about the great player who could individually perform at the highest levels, but couldn't or wouldn't make his teammates better. He was more concerned about a new contract or personal numbers than being a great leader.

Being a *great* husband isn't achieved overnight. Each of us has a choice every day to select maturity over immaturity, selflessness over selfishness, and wisdom over folly. The more often we make the right choices, the closer we get to greatness. Think about applying Jim Rohn's advice to make "measurable progress in a reasonable amount of time." What I am espousing is not unattainable or unrealistic because I'm not asking for perfection, but greatness from myself and from you. All around the world footage of Muhammad Ali's mantra, "I am the greatest" has been seen and engrained in our minds. Let it become your mantra in serving your wife and children.

CHAPTER 3

GAME CHANGERS

"A good hockey player plays where the puck is. A great hockey player plays where the puck is going to be".

–Wayne Gretzky

I love this quote from Wayne Gretzky because not only is it great hockey advice, but it is also great marital advice. Oftentimes, husbands function based on where they *think* their marriage is, not on a vision of where it actually is or should be headed. Husbands will fall short if their actions continue to be based on where they *think* their wife is a woman, mother, and workforce contributor.

In many of my counseling sessions, I have heard men say, "I want my wife to take on the traditional female role as mother, homemaker, cook, cleaner, and be there to satisfy my sexual needs. This is how it's always been." Not only is the wife's arms folded, she is shaking her head in disagreement because her husband's expectations are not in line with hers.

For generations, men have taken on traditional roles of working to provide for their families, addressing home and other necessary repairs, while providing overall love and protection for their families. In some respects, the "traditional roles" of a husband and wife are still employed by couples everywhere. I'm not espousing that we throw away the traditional roles all together, because with compromise, proper understanding and daily application, these marriages can be successful. However, husbands today have to be willing to make a "in game adjustments" as many wives desire and have achieved careers.

Women have greater expectations on men these days than their mothers and grandmothers did in previous generations. Thirty years ago, a wife wouldn't expect much assistance from her husband around the house or with the children because the societal paradigm charged her with those responsibilities. The husband was the primary breadwinner and maintained the physical structure of the home and mechanical work. Times have changed.

Wives today fully expect their husbands to be involved with the children, household chores, family functions, and still contribute economically for the family as in decades past. A number of wives desire their household responsibilities to function 50/50. During my pre-marital sessions there is a section entitled *Great Expectations*. Men still expect their future wives to cook, clean, take care of the children, and make the house a home. If the woman wants to work full-time, most of the men don't object to it, but it isn't always one of their primary expectations.

On the other hand, women in my pre-marital sessions always include in their *Great Expectations List* that their future husband will assist with cooking, cleaning, raising the children, financial provision, loving her and children, and handling all of the maintenance work. The majority of these women are educated and pursuing full-time careers. Another challenge for today's marriages is that it is becoming increasingly difficult to live on just one income from the husband while the wife stays home to raise the children. Women today have no alternative than to contribute to the household economically just like men. This is a major shift in the way families functioned over the last 20, 30, or 40 years.

Change on the Fly

"If you don't change, you will become extinct."
                                    -Spencer Johnson, MD

Embracing or adapting to change can be difficult. Allowing yourself to be open for change is necessary for growth and improvement. I believe it's part of the human DNA to be resistant to change. Most people resist change because they fear the unknown; which takes them out of their comfort zone. Change is inevitable, and if we as husbands don't make intentional efforts to change, the chances of happiness and success in our marriage will put Team Family in last place, and likely end in divorce.

Every year during the off-season, the NHL, NFL, NBA, MLB, or PGA may make slight or extensive changes to the rules of the game. When the new season arrives, the announcers cover the new changes in their pre-game introductions. As the game gets underway, there is always a player who operates under the old rules and gets penalized which hurts the entire team. It's not that the player is being defiant by refusing to adapt, instead, he has become so comfortable playing the game under the old rules (probably since he was a kid), that when the adrenaline kicks in and the clock starts, it's full breakaway mode. For some players, it may take a season to adapt to the new rule changes. The sooner they focus, practice and act in accordance with the new rules, the greater their team's chance of success.

Changing Family Structure

The ideal family structure of a husband/father and wife/mother in the home raising the children doesn't exist as often as it once did years ago. Very few adults in their 20's and 30's had positive, involved men in their home growing up who were both the husband and father. Most of my friends were raised in single-parent households, and some of them were raised by their fathers. Sadly, the current statistics provide us with alarming rates of children born out of wedlock, regardless of ethnicity, where the mother, not the father, is the head of household raising the children.

For my generation and this current one, there are several different types of homes in America, which have shaped the understanding of what is a great husband. We have children being raised by single mothers, single fathers, by parents who have decided to cohabitate rather than get married, by grandparents and uncles and aunts. We have more homes being headed by same-sex couples. There are too many variations of what a family looks like today that to describe all of them would be extremely difficult.

i. Societal changes: Male family role

What does this change in the traditional family structure mean for a husbands and wives today? The answer is simple: *Many men and women today (and probably in the future) either have a distorted or genuinely misinformed perspective of what a husband is actually supposed to be.*

The fact that many men and women grow up in homes without a husband/father is alarming. Many women were raised in homes that didn't have a husband and father, so they saw their mothers do everything-without the assistance of a man. In response to this environment, these women become ultra-independent and thus struggle with asking their husbands for help because they believe they can do everything on their own. Other women who were the product of a similar environment are determined to ensure that their husband doesn't turn out like their own absent or disengaged father and they refuse to live like their independent mothers. Such women demand full involvement and participation from their husbands. In both cases, these women want their husbands to be fully involved and be great men, but aren't totally sure what that really looks like.

The absence of a husband in the home has left men struggling to define this role for themselves. You may have heard people say, "You can only give what you have" or "You can only teach what you know." This is certainly true for men today who are now husbands. I have talked and counseled so many men who didn't have a father growing up as a child and it has left them deficient in the area of not only being a great husband to their wife, but father to their children.

In most cases, these men desire to be great husbands they just don't know what it looks like nor how to achieve it. We cannot underestimate the power of an involved, loving husband and father in the home to the life of a young boy. The opposite is unfortunately true as well. We cannot truly measure all of the devastating consequences of an absent husband and father in the home of the life of a young boy.

Due to these societal changes, coupled with the fact that men may struggle transitioning from being single to married, I have a suggestion to offer. I encourage every man, regardless if he had or didn't had a positive husband/father in the home to seek out male role models to challenge and inspire him to become great in every aspect of his life. Men need to surround themselves with men who are older and wiser than they are to motivate, inspire, challenge, and correct them to ensure they achieve greatness as a husband and in all other areas of their lives.

This challenge is easier said than done for most men. Ask a man who are his male best friends and they are often hard-pressed to rattle off four or five names. This often isn't true of women, who are much more skilled at maintaining friendships. Although men need friendship, we often don't have them or take time to cultivate the ones we do have. Furthermore, it is easier as a single man to maintain male friendships, but once a man gets married, he often focuses much if not all of his time to his wife and children. Little room is left in his mind and schedule for quality, consistent friendships and mentor relationships. New husbands are rookies and must seek out a veteran to learn the ropes of being great husbands.

ii. Blended families & In-Laws

Perhaps one of the biggest game-changers to marital relationships is the increasing reality of blended families. Before I ever helped a married couple navigate through the complexities of a blended family, I was part of one. As a child, I learned how to successfully navigate between two different worlds because my parents were divorced when I was 7 years old. There was dad's world and his family, while there was mom's world and her family. My sister and I became great at manipulating our different living environments.

When I do premarital counseling we always address the need to cut the cords of dependence and allegiance with our parents in order to align with our future spouse. This cutting of the cords of dependence and allegiance is also a task that blended families must endure as well, but from a different perspective. A great deal of marital strife occurs in blended families when one spouse is more aligned with their children than their spouse.

My mom understood this early on in her relationship with

my stepfather Cal, and she made the allegiance shift. My sister Sarah and I did not like it and wished it did not happen. I was initially disrespectful to Cal but over time I realized he was there to help us and not take anything away from our family. Cal also had three kids of his own. We learned early that Cal and my mom were not going to have multiple allegiances— there had to be one, between the two of them. All of us, their five children had to become second to the primary allegiance that Cal and Mom had as a married couple.

Unfortunately, some spouses have struggled making this allegiance shift. I have seen mothers and fathers who can never be too far away from their biological kids and grandkids. I've heard them say to their spouse, "my kids will always be first." Shifting allegiance is difficult and people think they have to choose their spouse over their kids as if one is more valuable or important than the other. That's not the issue because both are valuable and both are important, but both cannot be number one on the allegiance chart. When the proper allegiance is established, spouse first, children second, the natural order of life is allowed to flow and everyone in the family will ultimately benefit.

Blended families also need to cut the cord of parental dependence as well. When a parent has depended on their children for friendship, emotional support or spiritual growth, it can create an unhealthy barrier for the husband and wife to climb over. I have seen so many parents with young to adolescent children who have created a relationship with them to such degree that they depend on them for the constant support mentioned above. Being a single parent had put them in a place where sometimes the only people they could depend on were their children. Then they find a romantic partner in their new spouse and the transition from depending on their children for support to depending on their spouse can be difficult one for everyone involved. Ensuring that spouse's first find support in each other and then the children, will help to secure a stable blended family.

Men who become a husband in a blended family have some additional challenges as well. One of the challenges is the difference of opinion on how to raise the children the wife brought into the marriage. Women often desire to raise their children according to their own standards and beliefs and they want their husband to support those decisions. This can be contentious if those standards differ from the husband. If you find yourself in this situation here are few things to consider: i) Ensure every child is loved, cared for, protected, and valued; and ii) Ensure there is respect and order in the home and that chaos, disrespect, and anarchy does not rule the home.

In order to find a balance between these two responsibilities and honor the values and parenting styles of your wife with her children, you must decide on the non-negotiable rules. You and your wife must agree on what those rules are that will not be debatable. For instance, a non-negotiable may be children are not allowed to curse at their parents. If a child does this, it will be addressed immediately by either parent in ways that have been agreed upon by both parents. This also means that there is room for negotiable actions as well. These are areas where the non-biological parent gives the lead to the biological parent on how to address certain situations or concerns. Determining what are the non-negotiable and negotiable rules or actions in your home will provide a unified front and reduce arguments and misunderstandings as well.

Invariably, for men, not only have the rules and plays changed for us since becoming a husband, but the expectations and requirements to be a *great* husband will make change even more challenging, but certainly doable.

The Change Agent

With the expectations changing for men today, more and more husbands need to become effective change agents to transform and rebuild *Team Family* into championship contenders. *Great* husbands must continuously evolve to meet the needs of their wives. Not only does he need to have good peripheral vision, but he needs to have good downfield vision to see beyond the obvious and anticipate the unexpected. After counseling couples for more than 10 years, I've seen consistent themes emerge from men and women as it relates to their top needs. Below is a snapshot of the top five needs of wives, while the top five needs of husbands will be discussed in chapter 12. Your growth as a husband will be a great save in your marriage as you embrace and live out the various roles and expectations by ensuring that your wife's top needs are met.

#1 Security

Regardless of a woman's age, race, religious affiliation, or number of years married, the majority of women cited "security" within their top five needs. A wife wants to feel secure: emotionally, relationally, financially, and spiritually. When she lacks a sense of security she experiences distress, fear, or exudes greater amounts of tension. Although it may not be externally displayed to her husband, that feeling manifests itself in other ways, such as not being as open with him or not as willing to engage in intimacy. The more a husband can make his wife feel secure, the less conflict they'll have and the greater their marital happiness.

#2 Support

Wives often cite their need of emotional, mental, and spiritual support. They used words like "being cared for, accepted, feeling understood, given comfort and verbal praise." The ability of a man to support his wife is a key skill to acquire if he is going to become a great husband. Support isn't just hearing what they have to say and nodding in agreement, but being present with them as they articulate their experience. The challenge for most men is that they believe their efforts to fix situations or offer solutions to dilemmas is being supportive. Although it is, for a wife it is more than that. Another word for support can be comfort, which means to awaken strength in someone in order to restore their sense of usefulness. For many wives, they long for this definition of comfort to be provided by their husbands.

#3 Love

I thought this was going to be #1 on the list, but it came in third. Often phrases like "to feel loved, to be loved, to be desired, to be wanted, were used to describe this need of love. From a Christian perspective, husbands are to love their wives as Christ loved the Church. (EN) It is described as a sacrificial love where we are to nourish and cherish them. When husbands *cherish* their wives they value and protect them. When he *nourishes* her, he helps her to develop her skills, dreams, and purpose.

#4 Communication

Wives listed direct communication and listening as a critical need. We all know that women are more verbal than men. This isn't news, nor is it news that most husbands are told they need to do a better job at listening. I don't think men necessarily have an issue with listening per se. Our problem is really found in our attention span. When husbands were dating and courting their future wives they were totally paying attention to every word and action in an effort to secure her companionship and love. After marriage, the husband's attention dwindles and gets divided with work, the children and other interests and activities. If men *worked* at paying attention to their wives again, it would directly improve their listening and communication skills. I recently read a great quote that said, *"The death of communication is the birthplace of resentment."* The moment we stop communicating, stop listening, or stop paying attention while our spouse talks, will be the very moment we birth resentment in them.

#5 Affection

Wives desire physical affection from their husbands without the ulterior motive of sex. They want to receive hugs and kisses, holding hands, and having their husband's undivided attention. They don't want their husband on the cell phone, watching TV, or surfing the Internet. They just want to spend quality time with him. Most husbands would agree that they could offer more affection without any motives for sex. I encourage you to increase your efforts to be affectionate, and watch your wife respond towards you in more positive ways.

Scoring Points

The Hat Trick

Now that you have a working list of the top five needs of wives as a template, you can quickly become a *great* husband by performing a hat trick: scoring three goals in the same night. After dinner and the kids are asleep, use this list to spark a dialogue with your wife by asking her the questions below. The goal is to gauge where your wife is at this moment in your marriage. Additionally, make sure you find out where she sees the relationship going in the future.

1. Do you agree with this top five list? Are these your top five needs? If not, what would be on your list?

2. When it comes to Security, how have I made you feel secure in this marriage? What are the things that I've done to cause you to not have a sense of security?

3. What is the most important way I could offer or provide support to you? What could I do immediately to meet this need of support?

Now is your time to take your shot at the open net and watch your abilities as a change agent soar to its potential. Your path to being a great husband will create defining moments in your marriage.

CHAPTER 4

STAYING INBOUNDS

"The best ability is availability."

-Trent Dilfer

Trent Dilfer often uses this quote in reference to football players staying healthy so that they can remain on the field to help their team win. I think it is also applicable for this chapter on "Staying Inbounds" in our marriage. Regardless of the sport, whether indoors or outdoors, there are boundaries and settings that determine what is inbounds and what is out-of-bounds. Players of any sport want to remain inbounds at all times and stay in flow of the game. Once that player is out of bounds, the play immediately stops. The game cannot continue until the player steps back in bounds.

In our marriages, we want to do our best to remain inbounds with our wives. The more we find ourselves out of bounds, it's an indication we may be out of touch, out of connection, out of communication, or out of intimacy with our wife.

Out of Bounds

i. Selfishness

"You can never be happily married to another until you get a divorce from yourself."

-Jerry McCant

One of the most common things that take men out of bounds is selfishness. When we are selfish in any area of life it usually negatively impacts our relationship with our wives. I'm not saying husbands shouldn't have time to themselves or activities they do that is just for them. Nor am I saying that a husband needs to be a pushover, someone without a spine who appeases his wife's dysfunctional or unhealthy behaviors. When I say selfishness I'm talking about the times when we are only focused on our needs, wants, desires, interests, and feelings, at the expense of others regardless of the impact. The "it's all about me" attitude will take us out of bounds with our wives every time.

The key to a successful marriage requires a conscious "death" to self. I've actually been proclaiming a similar analogy: weddings are like funerals and funerals are like weddings. When you attend a wedding the bride and groom are uniting their life together and are actually dying to self. Thus, as a guest, you witnessed the death of self. I imagine you probably wore black! As for funerals, in the Christian religion, whenever someone dies they are reunited with their Savior Jesus Christ to spend eternity with Him. Although the funeral marks the death of a life on this Earth, it is actually the uniting of a soul to their Creator, a wedding of two beings.

When you got married, your focus should have shifted from your own interests to the interests of your wife.[5] It is important to continually remind yourself of the wedding vows you took and make a conscious effort to live by that commitment. This is something that I recommend husbands do throughout their marital life. Although I am a proponent of the traditional wedding vows, it certainly isn't uncommon for couples today to write their own. But since we can't possibly mention all of the variations in vows, allow me to provide one of the more common ones:

"I Jacob take thee Rachel to have and to hold from this day forward, for better or for worse, for richer or for poorer, in sickness and in health, to love and to cherish; from this day forward until death do us part."

Meditate on these words and remember that fateful day when they were spoken. Allow them to be your assessment of how you are doing in regards to dying to self and allowing *selflessness* to be your guide as a husband. If there is an area you need to improve upon (as we all do), don't create excuses or justifications, but rather search for the solutions to improve and then begin implementing them.

ii. Complacency

The next trick play that takes us out of bounds as husbands is the tendency to become complacent. Men were not complacent when they were dating and courting their future wife.

We were attentive, kind, assertive, and focused on our future wife as we continued to gain yards through the dating and engagement process. We would do things that were normally outside of our personality and character in order to win the heart of our future wife. We said all the right things and had the best of intentions. For most of us, after we return from the honeymoon, our focus shifts to work, career, making money, providing for the family, and eventually spending time with the kids. It's not that we don't love our wife anymore, it's just that we can become complacent with keeping our focus on the *things* our wives need to be happy.

Our focus is now divided between several things and we neglect doing the thoughtful stuff that caused our wife to fall in love with us in the first place. The weight of the everyday can cause us to become complacent with our affection, love, attention, and quality time with her. Unfortunately, if we neglect something long enough, it will begin to drift off course or worse, deteriorate. If there is one thing every wife wants from her husband, it is for her to know without a shadow of doubt that she is his number one priority.

iii. Laziness

The challenge of laziness, or to state it in another way, doing the bare minimum to get by, plagues even good husbands. For some of them, throughout their lives, some men have been able to get by doing the bare minimum. They show great promise, but never fully live up to their potential. When I see this characteristic in men while conducting marital counseling sessions, it is a personality trait that has been with them their entire life. Very rarely is a man not lazy before getting married and then after marriage *becomes* lazy. This tendency to do the bare minimum frustrates wives because they see all the potential in their husband and they can't understand why he won't fulfill it. Wives are even more frustrated when they see their husbands go above and beyond and perform tasks that are important to them, but will never go to such great lengths for things that are important to her. Laziness truly takes a husband out of bounds with his wife and it often takes time before she is willing to allow him back in the game.

iv. Personal compass

Men are often out of bounds when they ignore their own emotional, psychological, and spiritual disposition. All of these personal tendencies are proportionately related to your health, commitment and stability. When we are struggling with these areas or have been neglecting them, it is impossible to be a great husband. We'll cover these areas in more depth in chapter 10. However when a man is unable or unwilling to lead himself properly, it causes his wife to lose her trust in him. The husband's decision "not lead himself well" usually causes situations in which the man is deemed to be untrustworthy. This lack of trust is compounded by the reality that wives often have a hard time trusting their husbands in these particular areas:

1. Emotions

Many women don't trust that their husbands care about or even know how to handle their emotions. They don't trust that their initial request for comfort and understanding will be understood and supported. Therefore, most women don't say anything and keep it bottled up inside until they cannot hold it any longer. Finally, when wives hit their breaking point, and express their emotions, it becomes overwhelming for their husbands, and hinders him from opening up this "touchy" discussion in the future.

2. Their Bodies/Sex

I have often heard from women that they don't trust their husband with their bodies. These women's experiences with sex have been that their husbands have their needs fulfilled, while the wives' needs or desires are secondary, or worse, ignored. Some of these same women are honest enough to say that they have their own insecurities about their bodies and sex, so when that is coupled with unsatisfactory sexual experiences with their husbands, their difficulty trusting that it will eventually be *their turn* is heightened.

3. Taking the Initiative & Completing Assignments

Several, women don't trust that their husbands will initiate and then plan a special event for them or the family. I hear this one often. Wives have said that if it benefits their husband directly, or it's something he's passionate about, then he will initiate and plan it down to the very last detail. Then she'll look at me in the counseling session and say, "but I don't feel that way when it comes to our marriage. I just don't trust that he'll take the initiative and plan things for the family or us because he's never done it!"

4. Money

When a wife doesn't trust her husband with money, it could be that she is the saver and he is a spender. The most common financial picture I see is that the wife is managing the household finances while the husband is disinterested in the process. Many women don't like this entire burden being placed on them. So if your wife is handing all of the finances, and you are aware of the stress she is under, offer to at least take a look at the bills and see if there is anything you can do to alleviate her stress.

Being out of bounds with your wife is the same as being out of order with God's design for the husband in the family.

In Bounds Points

Success on so many levels and in various arenas, such as relationships, sports, and the workplace, is achieved by staying in bounds. It doesn't mean that you have to play it safe all the time, but by using creativity, initiative, and prudence you will rack up points with your wife in the long run. Here are a few good strategies which will keep you in bounds.

i. Team Unity

When a team has come to mutual agreement to put their egos and personal agendas aside, to remain united and committed as a team, it will be difficult to defeat them, regardless of their respective individual talent level. A team of players all operating from the same page in the playbook, with the discipline to fulfill their role and function in the moment, is a beautiful thing to witness. Teams that function this way capture our heart because they are a physical illustration of selfless play leading to success.

However, when we see a team lack unity, when they don't trust each other, or when there is dissention in the ranks, it ultimately kills their chances of success. It doesn't matter how talented each player is individually, if they can't get on the same page, the agony of defeat is inevitable.

Is there unity on *Team Family*? Are you and your wife both on the same page by putting your egos and personal agendas aside? When teams lack unity, the first place we look to is the leadership and the game plan. As husbands, our job is to provide leadership and be able to create a game plan. The more we function in our role as the leader of the family or Team Captain, the easier it will be for our wife to buy in to the plan and be on our team.

Leadership is earned not because of talent alone, but by dependability, likeability, and having a mindset that the team comes first. The best leaders will also have a game plan for the opponents they face. As husbands, we are challenged to have a game plan for how our relationship with our wife will be maintained and cultivated over the years. We need a game plan to ensure our long-term financial success. We need a game plan for how we will raise our children. We also need a game plan for our personal, marital, spiritual and emotional growth.

Great leaders are also willing to make in-game adjustments from the input of those on the team to move the team closer to its goal of winning. A great husband will welcome and solicit input from his wife as to the in-game adjustments that need to be made. Our wives have a wealth of experience, knowledge, insight, creativity, and energy, that we need to draw upon. Embracing those attributes allows our marriage to be success-ful, and *Team Family* wins far more often than it loses.

ii. Focus

Our focus as husbands directly influence how we think, act, and communicate with our wives. The greatest athletes practice with laser-like focus, which is centered on winning. They don't allow outside media influences to deter them from their ulti-mate goal. Their ability to focus with diligence is often what separated them from both the good and average players. As husbands, this scenario is no different for us.

We have a variety of things that we can choose to focus on like our wives' negative characteristics, berate the things she has not done, the mistakes she has made, and compile a list of the broken promises. Instead, you should choose to focus on all of the positive and life-affirming attributes of your wife. Again, I'm not saying to ignore dysfunctional or abusive behav-ior. Yet our willingness to focus on the right things at the right time can lead to marital success.

One of things I do to help me stay focused on the right things is that I kept two different journals. In one journal, every day I write down the wisdom or activities of the day that I've experienced to help me be the best man I can possibility be. I no longer rely on my memory to keep all of the insight into my own thoughts and behaviors. Writing it down allows me to go back and refresh myself later.

The second journal is where I write about my appreciation and gratitude for my wife. Each day, I write down at least one thing I value or appreciate about her or zero in on what she did for the family or our children. I learned some time ago that if I spend my time focusing on any grievances I have about my wife, it blinds me to all of the attributes and actions that I truly love about her and am grateful for. In many respects, our grievance list doesn't necessarily go away because we are human and will make mistakes. There is no such thing as "human perfection." Pick up a journal today or download an app on your smartphone and start working on your gratitude list and it will change your focus.

iii. Huddling Up: Communication

Many NFL teams are running the No Huddle Offense in an attempt to run as many plays as possible to wear out the defense. Under ideal circumstances, the No Huddle Offense is an effective strategy. Yet when the offense can't convert first downs, the entire No Huddle strategy fails. It puts continuous unnecessary pressure on the defense to perform because of the offense's failure.

When the No Huddle stops working, teams go back to huddling up. They make sure everyone is on the same page by chewing up the clock to give their defense a chance to rest. Furthermore, it gives the quarterback the time to communicate the right plays in the huddle which is crucial for success.

In our marriages, if we aren't careful, our communications with our wife can mirror the No Huddle Offense. We are living and working at a fast pace because there is so much to accomplish in one day. This eventually leads to a breakdown in communication which may lead to disappointment, anger, frustration, and failure. Of course, we all have different communication styles and different ways of comprehending what is being spoken, but that shouldn't deter us from clearly and consistently communicating with our wives. If our wives have to be the ones who always huddle us up to talk about an issue, this will become problematic in the marriage. It's no secret that most women are more verbal than men, but that doesn't excuse us from lack of effort in this area.

I like to consider communication as more of a game of "catch" rather than a game of volleyball as it has often been described. In volleyball, the goal is to hit the ball back over the net as soon as it crosses our side of the court. Do you ever find yourself doing this when you are communicating with your wife? When she is talking to you, you're gearing yourself up to say what's on your mind as soon as she is finished. By responding in this manner, you are not truly listening to understand, but rather waiting for your time to talk.

In your next conversation with your wife, try really hard to think about the game of catch. When she throws the ball at you, your job is to hold on to it and then throw it back.

Could you imagine how much better off our marriages would be if husbands took the time to truly catch what our wives are saying, embrace it, and then respond with a genuine communication from the heart? Always remember that your goal is to be the MVP of *Team Family*, and not the recipient of your wife's selective hearing award.

It's also important to mention that men are usually more direct in their communication with their spouse, yet they don't want their spouse using the same direct method in responding. To alleviate the tension, choose your words carefully *before* you speak. If the issue is sensitive, then take time to address it later when you have had more time to reflect. I have found that sometimes delay or silence is best because it give us time to process what we are thinking and feeling and then come up with the most appropriate and considerate way of conveying it to our wife so she hears us.

Great husbands listen to what is being said by their wives, rather than interjecting how they feel about what is being said. Make an effort to be attentive to the way the communication is being delivered. Consider your wife's tone, body language, and facial expression. Always try to ask clarifying questions rather than give defensive responses. When we focus on understanding, rather than confronting perceived indictments and judgments, the opportunity for mutual agreement and teamwork leads to marital success.

Lastly, in terms of communication, two of the most powerful words in the English language are "I'm sorry." These two words can cause a change in the trajectory of your marriage and help remove the penalties stored in your wife's heart from past pain, hurt, and disappointment, as a result of a conflict in communication.

How's Your Film Study?

"Jim, by now you ought to have a Ph.D. in your wife."

-Former Counselor

Every week NFL players spend time in film study before their next game. The purpose of film study is to see where they made mistakes and where they achieved success. This is not a time to watch highlights, instead, they are looking to see which plays worked and which ones did not. Coaches are pondering whether the play failed because of lack of talent, lack of execution, or a combination of the two. Watching themselves on film helps players get better for future games.

Players are also given tape of their opponent's last few games to understand their opponent's tendencies, strengths, and weaknesses. The more film they watch, the more they know about their opponent and how to mentally and physically prepare a game plan to expose weaknesses, and win the game. This same visual strategy is applicable in your daily life as husband and wife.

The sooner you become a student of your own strengths, weaknesses, and tendencies, the closer you will be to becoming a *great* husband. You need to study what causes one thing to work well with your wife and what doesn't work at all. Just as important, you need to be a student of your wife. Spend time observing her actions, listening to her words, and reading her body language. The more time you spend in the film study of your wife, the more you will understand how to minimize her weaknesses and maximize her strengths.

There was a time when my wife and I were in marriage counseling. Yes, that's right, a marriage counselor in marriage counseling! It was tough to swallow but I knew I needed another perspective on what was causing the both of us sheer frustration. At one point in the session, the counselor turned, looked at me and said, "Jim, by now you ought to have a PhD in your wife." I was embarrassed and shocked. The worse part was that he was right. My wife and I had been together for several years, and by now I should have been an expert on all things pertaining to her.

As I sat there, I realized that I had a bachelor's degree in my wife. It was now time that I worked towards earning my Ph.D. The only way to get there was by increasing my film study. I encourage you to increase your film study of your wife to keep you in bounds and playing at your highest levels as teammates on the most important team, *Team Family*.

SECOND QUARTER

CHAPTER 5:

Distractions and Difficulties

"The game of life is a lot like football. You have to tackle your problems, block your fears, and score your points when you get the opportunity."

-Lewis Grizzard

Every team has to fight through distractions and difficulties. The great teams, the ones that win championships, not only fight through distractions and difficulties, but thrive because their intensity and determination to succeed. Their drive to win increases rather than withers under the pressure of public scrutiny. A distraction is something that is usually not related to play on the field, but it takes up much of the attention of the team because everyone outside of the team is talking about it. For example, a common distraction is a star player holding out of training camp for a larger contract, or a player making inappropriate comments that are immediately picked up by the media.

Like distractions, difficulties can cause contending teams their entire season if they don't unite and make a commitment to work harder. A difficulty is something usually related to play on the field. An example of a difficulty is a star player such as the team quarterback, sustaining a season ending injury, or the hiring of new head coach implementing a completely different system than the previous coach. Again, if the team doesn't handle a distraction or difficulty correctly, it can derail their entire season.

As husbands, we will no doubt be faced with distractions and difficulties in our marriages that will come from both inside and outside our households. Distractions will always be there, however, the goal is to do your best to keep them to a minimum and think before you act or speak. Just like sports teams, if we spend too much time in our marriage focusing on the distractions, it can derail the entire relationship. The focus should be figuring out ways to win with your wife in spite of the distraction. The difficulties in the lives of professional athletes can sabotage their career. As married men, distractions can be the end of their marriage if they don't respond to them correctly.

It's not that we can't overcome the difficulties. The real question is whether we are willing to do what's necessary to succeed in spite of the difficulty. How you handle these distractions and difficulties will often determine your immediate and long-term success. Like today's great quarterbacks who wear a "cheat sheet" of plays on their wrist, you'll also need your own cheat sheet, to remind you of the pitfalls to avoid on your path to becoming *great* husbands.

Distractions: Your Blind Spots

Your physical health: This is a distraction both in a positive and negative sense. We can be overly focused on our physical health where we exercise and care for our bodies to the point that it takes first priority in our life; the fitness fanatic. The other side of the health coin is that we may be experiencing sickness, disease, or injury, that we become so focused on it, our emotional, spiritual, and mental state succumbs to depression and self-pity. Both of these extremes will rob us of focusing on the larger goal of being a *great* husband to our wife.

Your children: It may seem harsh, but our children can become a distraction. We can show more love and spend more time with the kids than we do our wives. Husbands can talk for hours with their wives about needs of the kids, yet never consider talking with their wives about the state of their marriage or checking in with her to see how she's doing personally. Granted, I am totally all for being a great father, what I'm not for, is using the children to hide from our first and foremost responsibility of being a *great* husband.

Your job: We can obtain so much admiration and applause on our jobs to the point where it becomes central to our identity. We will do whatever it takes to succeed at work, but won't apply that same effort to succeed in our marriage. Of course, you need to offer your best at work, since they are compensating you and that directly impacts your family, however, make sure you "work" on finding a balance between your job and the needs of your wife.

Other beautiful women: Women are by far a big distraction for men. There will always be beautiful women in this world. Wherever you go, you will see a woman more beautiful than the last one you gazed upon. Then you start to fantasize what it would like to be married to the one from yesterday or the day before. Should we have chosen that waitress over our wife? Absolutely not! Every minute that is spent wondering about another beautiful woman is one less minute you have to devote to understanding and loving your own wife. Fantasies are not real!

Your economic status: Several men have told me in marriage counseling that they don't have to time to focus on their wife or the marriage because their economic situation is in terrible shape. As if to say, "I don't have any more mental or emotional energy to give to my wife right now, because all of my focus is on making money for the family." I understand the noble position of wanting to improve your economic condition, yet that cannot be used as your rationalization for putting your husband responsibilities on the shelf for an extended period of time. By the time you get around to improving your economic problem, you'll have a much bigger problem because your wife will feel disconnected and abandoned. Don't let your economic state rob you from focusing on winning with your wife first. Enlist the help of friends and family to allow you to spend quality time with your wife and plan inexpensive date nights like when you were dating or schedule weekday lunches with her.

Personality Clashes

I have counseled men who were honestly trying the best they could to love, cherish, protect, and provide for their wife, but for various reasons, she wasn't keeping her end of the marital agreement.

* *Negativity:* A wife with a negative disposition may have become negative over the course of the marriage or already had a negative disposition before you ever met her. She sees negativity in any situation. This is a woman who is actually negative about her own future, your marriage, your children, and life in general. What makes being married to a wife with a negative disposition so challenging is that her negative words can cut you to the core as a man and strike a blow to your ego. Her negative disposition will drain your enthusiasm and hope for the future. Often times, your initial response will be anger, but that will soon turn into bitterness. The longer you are angry and bitter towards your wife, the more difficult it becomes to love and protect her. Most of us would rather be away from her and by ourselves than spend any time with her [6].

There are three possible solutions if you find yourself married to a woman with a negative disposition. First, if she wasn't a negative person when you married her, then chances are something in your marriage has brought on this negativity. This is actually good news because it means that you have a chance to work on restoring and repairing the relationship. Her negativity should eventually decrease and you'll once again have the woman you initially fell in love with.

However, if she has always had a negative disposition since

you've known her, then you have to realize that no matter how *great* of a husband you become, if she doesn't work on her own personal issues, her negative disposition will never go away. This doesn't give you the green light to stop being responsible and trying to be a *great* husband. It means that your attempts to change her begin with praying that God would heal those aspects of her personality that only He can reach. It also means that you don't have to carry the burden of her negativity any longer. She may choose to remain negative, but you will no longer allow her negative disposition to ruin *your* mood and emotions.

Thirdly, you may need to see her through a different lens. There is an origin to this negativity and when you know the origin of it, you can see her through a lens of compassion and understanding. Has she been abused in the past? Deeply hurt? Being married to a wife with a negative disposition is certainly a difficulty, but one that you can overcome with thoughtfulness, prayer, and change in perspective.

Controlling: A wife with a controlling disposition is a person who needs to have control over every aspect of your life. She wants to be in control of the money, the family calendar, your personal calendar, how much time you spend with your family and friends, and what you do on a daily basis. Sometimes a wife is controlling out of a deep sense of fear and anxiety about the future. Her motive for being controlling is to keep things safe and predictable. She may be controlling because of trauma and loss that she's been through. She mistakenly believes that if *she* were in control of things, then she won't get hurt or you won't leave her. Other times, wives are controlling because they are immature, self-centered, and manipulative. Wives with controlling dispositions have extreme difficulty being vulnerable and trusting someone else to handle things. They feel threatened if you desire to be your own person and have your own way of doing things.

Identifying the reason for your wife's controlling disposition will dictate the actions you need to take to be a *great* husband. If her controlling comes from fear and anxiety, then make a concentrated effort to do things together that demonstrates she can trust you. Trust is a major hurdle for women with controlling dispositions, so it is important for you to remain true to our word, follow through when needed, and work and always remind her that the two of you are an unstoppable team. Your actions are likely to decrease her fear and anxiety, thereby lessening her controlling nature.

However, if your wife is controlling because of past trauma and pain, then convincing her to seek individual counseling will improve things. It's also a great idea to go to counseling as a couple, to help heal the past traumas and give you greater insight into her struggles.

Finally, if your wife is controlling because of a lack of maturity and character development, then you've married a person who is broken on the inside. She may even have a personality disorder. Addressing this type of person often requires extensive individual and couples counseling, because it will not go away in a few days. Furthermore, as you grow and become more responsible, more mature, and more thoughtful, it may initially make matters worse. Your growth will be a direct mirror to her of her non-growth. She may become even more dysfunctional. However, love does cover a multitude of sins and as you remain steadfast in your love for her and pray for her personal growth, there is the strong possibility that she will change.[7] Always remember that you should be praying for your wife so that God can do the work that you cannot. Allow Him to send the right people who can heal the areas that you can never reach.

Never Enough: The wife who carries a *never enough* disposition is the type of woman who no matter what you give her, nor how much you change, nor what lengths you go through to make her happy, it will never be enough. She always wants more and is never satisfied. Unfortunately, these types of wives are very hard to please and more than likely demonstrated this type of disposition during the dating and engagement period.

Many men overlook this characteristic and welcome it during the dating phase. They view it as a challenge and test of their manhood, to prove they could win the love and affection of this type of woman. Yet, after a man marries this type of woman, her *never enough* disposition gets old real fast. What was once something that he used to strengthen his ego, now deflates or demoralizes it because he realizes she'll never be truly happy or satisfied.

Figuring out the reasons why your wife has a *never enough* disposition will help you not take things personally and allows you to see the events in her life that got her to where she is now. This understanding, like with many of the others mentioned, shifts our lens with compassion, grace or new perspective. Pray for her and ask God to help her mature and learn the art of being content and grateful for what she has. The *never enough* wife hasn't learned this yet, but once she does, your marriage will blossom and you'll be even more motivated to be a *great* husband for her.

It's Never Good Enough: The wife who displays the *it's never good enough* disposition, is similar to the *never enough* wife, and can have similar traits of negativity as well. This is the wife that no matter how hard you try to do the right things or complete tasks for her, she says, "it's never good enough!" You think you've done a great job but she'll find all of the things that you did wrong or that weren't completed to her satisfaction. A wife with this disposition often points out the deficiencies in a way that suggests she is never happy with anything *you* do. She may not be as negative as the wife with the negative attitude, but when she constantly points out all the things you do wrong, it will be seen by you, as negative. The *it's never good enough wife* will push her husband to say things like, "Screw it! No matter how hard I try she'll never be happy. What's the point?" This is the husband that has decided he is not leaving the marriage, but he is not bending over backwards for her anymore. In other words, he may be there physically, but he has left the marriage emotionally and psychologically.

The *it's never good enough wife* is often like the *never enough wife*, in that appreciation and gratitude don't flow easily from her lips. When a man is married to an *it's never good enough* wife, who also has the ability to continuously show gratitude and appreciation, it is actually a good thing for a husband. It's good because she can be content, but know there is more in her husband that he can accomplish. She can actually help to push him to being a *great* husband because he won't have the space to be complacent and settle. However, if the *never good enough* attitude does not show gratitude and appreciation it will push her husband further away from his greatness.

As husbands, we have to be able to identify the areas that she has honestly and accurately pointed out that need to be improved upon. Once we come to terms with this truth, it our job to become better in those areas. At the same time, we have to know when we have gotten better and be proud of our growth, while not allowing our wife's constant push for more to demoralize us. There comes a time when you realize you have made the improvements and now she is just being unfair. Being able to come to terms with that dynamic is key to your success if you're married to a woman with the *it's never good enough* attitude.

Withholding Sex: The wife who is withholding sex from her husband may be doing this for a few reasons. First, she may feel insecure about her own body and sexuality. Over time, this may have become a byproduct of her unwillingness, coupled with her religious upbringing that didn't talk about sex. She probably grew up in a home that viewed sex as dirty and only for procreation.

Second, sometimes these women grew up in homes where they were told that only "loose" women enjoy sex and it degrades their bodies. If this is where your wife is regarding sex, then the remedy is to seek a sex counselor who shares your wife's same faith or religion. It also helps when your wife is able to connect with an older married woman who shared that same religious upbringing. This older woman can provide a different perspective that says sex is meant to be an enjoyable experience between a husband and wife.

Third, a wife may be withholding sex because experiences with her husband has shown her that it is a one-sided exchange. Her husband is physically satisfied and her needs are neglected or ignored. She withholds sex from her husband because she does not want to feel like a piece of meat for his satisfaction. She is hurt, disheartened and disappointed. She feels neglected and used. If this applies to you and your wife, you must immediately apologize to her for the narrative that you have created which tells her that sex is only about *you*! The healing begins and continues when you make a conscious effort to meet her needs before the intimacy of the sexual act occurs. Once it starts, you do your best to make it about her and not about *you*. Even if this means that you are not completely satisfied at the end of the intimacy.

Fourth, a wife may be withholding sex as punishment due to her husband's misdeeds or failures. She withholds sex out of anger and manipulation. She uses it as a tool to get him to do the things she wants. Out of the three reasons mentioned previously, this is usually the most destructive in a marriage because it creates bitterness in the husband. When sex moves from a time of intimacy to sex to being a power struggle, it creates more strife. Intense marriage counseling or sex therapy will be required, as there is a pattern that has been created between the two of you that cannot be fixed on your own. Again, seeking outside help is definitely needed because more than likely there are a lot more problems going on outside the bedroom than inside the bedroom.

Emotionally Unstable: If you are married to a woman with an emotionally unstable disposition, it may be connected to a legitimate mental illness. She may be broken inside and incidents of past trauma, pain, and abuse will play out on you as the husband each time something happens. She may become unstable and love you one moment and hate you the next. On Sunday she wants to be married to you, on Monday she wants a divorce. Don't become frustrated and write her off completely, because there are increasing numbers of individuals suffering from legitimate mental illnesses like depression, bipolar disorder, or schizophrenia. All of these illnesses require outpatient treatment options that include medication, group and individual therapy.

To be a *great* husband to a wife diagnosed with a mental illness is a completely different set of dynamics because it is not her fault. Although mental illness is a painful stigma to bear, it does not have to be categorically viewed as this is who she is for the rest of her life. As a *great* husband, you should view her mental illness on a continuum of recovery, with the hope that healing is possible, especially since there are several treatment options and resources to help both of you achieve stability.

It is important to know that countless men and women who have been diagnosed with mental illness go on to lead successful, happy lives. *Great* husbands must show a lot of love, support, and patience. They must understand that this is a journey that will have lots of relapses, replays and ups and downs. A *great* husband will see the need to obtain personal counseling to deal with his own anger and frustration with life and God. He will need a professional to help him process all of his complex emotions and to bounce things off of as he struggles with unanswered questions like, "Of all the people with mental illness, why does my wife have to be the one? " "Why do I have to deal with this?" Mental illness is real, but remember that it's not the person's fault and sometimes their actions are unintentional.

Unavailable: An unavailable wife is cold and distant and just doesn't want to be bothered. For a variety of reasons some are just downright mean and nasty, and it has nothing to do with their husband. Others are so hurt and disappointed by the pain in the marriage, that she is just completely done. She has checked out and is physically present but no longer emotionally, spiritually, psychologically, or sexually present, because there is too much pain. I've counseled many women who have said, "Pastor Jim I am just numb. I can't feel anything. I have no joy. I have no more tears left." Chances are, the problems occurred over a significant period of time without any intervention. A therapist now has to peel back multiple layers to get the root of the pain. For other women, their temperament is such that they may not like being touched often and would prefer that physical expressions of love are kept to a minimum. This can be problematic if the husband enjoys showing continuous physical affection. Again, with proper counseling both of you can grow by understanding the differences and dynamics of your relationship.

Sickness/disability: When a wife has a disability or an illness that hinders her ability to live or work, it can put a tremendous strain on the relationship. Her disability or illness does not allow her to care for herself the way she desires and she may not be able to care for her husband either. It places the husband in the primary position of care-taker and other aspects of the relationship such as sex, companionship, and travel, which all have to be put on hold or reduced significantly.

When the wife is doing her best to improve her health or make the most of the life despite the disability, the easier it is for the husband to bear the weight of care-taker and do so in a loving, patient fashion. Sometimes though, the sickness or disability is such that depression or self-pity settles into her heart and she doesn't do the necessary things to improve or stay engaged in life. These are difficult moments for the husband, because if he is not careful, it can create frustration in him, which can turn into bitterness, leading to lack of patience and understanding.

A husband will know he is in those moments when he begins to doubt the level of illness or disability she is experiencing. When he starts to think it's more in her head than it is an actual illness. In order to keep this from happening and to remain a loving, patient care-taker, I would recommend a few action steps.

First, take care of yourself so that you can continue to take care of your wife. Don't stop working out, eating right, and finding time for friends and family. Second, maintain your relationship with God because you will need the strength to care for her and the faith to believe that she can be healed or in the absence of total healing still be able to enjoy life to its fullest. Third, seek individual or group counseling because over time you may experience compassion fatigue. By having an individual therapist or group you can confide in allows you to process your experiences properly so you can continue in your care-taking role.

Abuse: Most of the time, when we think of domestic violence or abuse, it is usually in the direction of the husband being the abuser and the wife is the victim. However, there are men who are being abused by their wife whether it's emotional, physical, or psychological. These men very often suffer in silence. Many think that no one will believe them, *What? You're a man, how could your wife abuse you?* Since this is a common reaction, these men never seek help. For other men, their egos get in the way and they don't want to be seen by others as being weak or a punk, so they suffer silently. If your wife is abusing you, then it is important for you to seek the same kind of help women do when they are in similar situations. There are resources available to help in these moments so that you don't suffer in silence. Never think you're less than a man because you're in this situation, and don't think you can fix the problem by yourself. Professional help is available and it's up to you to let someone know what's happening, so that they can walk you through the process.

Choosing Perseverance

"Winners never quit and quitters never win."

-Vince Lombardi

The distractions and difficulties discussed here are common experiences many couples face. If we believe that our marriages will never go through distractions or be confronted with difficulties, we are operating under an unrealistic expectation. Every marriage has its periods of difficulties and distress.[8] Some are harder than others to overcome, but if we have perseverance, our chances of success increase significantly. Perseverance is usually one of the main reasons for achieving long term happiness as a couple.

In order to persevere, we must have a realistic understanding of the dynamics of our marriage. This will create a clear picture of what is and what is not present with your wife. Living in that reality will enable you to keep an undying commitment to becoming the very best husband you can be. There has never been a team in the history of sports that refused to play after halftime because they were losing by a ridiculous amount. Regardless of the score, they all showed up to play the rest of the game. Despite the score, still come out and play with perseverance. May the words of Bruce Arians encourage you in moments of doubt, "Tough times don't last, but tough people do."

CHAPTER 6:

WINNING AT WORK

"Hard work beats talent when talent doesn't work hard".

-**Kevin Durant**

Those of us who weren't gifted or fortunate enough to play sports for a living, often dream of what it must be like to get paid for a playing a game. We travel to our day job listening to sports talk radio and wish we were driving to the practice facility of our favorite team, rather than our place of employment. Most of us fail to realize that professional athletes are just like us. We all have to put in a 9-to-5, answer to a boss, follow company policy, and do things we may not like doing. Yet, we acquiesce to receive our paycheck. Muhammad Ali viewed his boxing career as a job that he got paid to do. It was up to him to perfect his boxing ability, and he had no problem" getting paid to beat up people." The harder he worked at that skill, the better he got at it, the more money he made and the more success he had. Kevin Durant continuously works hard during the off-season in order step up his game every time he is on the court. Both Muhammad Ali and Kevin Durant are individual examples of winning at work.

Most recently, we've been privileged to watch a sports team demonstrate a tremendous amount of talent and work ethic at the same time. The 2015 Golden State Warriors began the season as defending NBA champions. Rather than coasting through the season, they returned to the court with an even greater intensity, work ethic, and teamwork. They broke the NBA record for starting the season with the most consecutive wins at 24. During the winning streak Interim Head Coach Luke Walton, was interviewed on Mike and Mike in the Morning on ESPN radio. Coach Walton was assuming the role of Head Coach in Steve Kerr's absence. Coach Walton described a team that was just as committed this year as they were last year. He also stated that the fingerprints of Coach Kerr's work ethic, practice time and game day preparations still influenced the team. It is tough to beat any team with this level of commitment, including *Team Family*, that not only has great talent, but a great work ethic as well.

Work Can Affect Home

It's no secret that men can derive a lot of satisfaction and self-worth from their careers. At the same time, a man's occupation can also be the source of frustration, bitterness, and anger. Men who find their work enjoyable, meaningful and financially rewarding, are often in a better place to be a *great* husband. These men experience a greater sense of peace and purpose in their lives and thus bring this same state of mind back home to their wives. However, men who are not fulfilled in their careers and don't make enough money to support their families, may have a difficult time being a *great* husband. Problems and salary dissatisfaction on the job can easily spill over into problems at home.

On the flip side of the coin, having satisfaction in your career doesn't guarantee success at being a *great* husband. There are plenty of men whose careers are thriving because it is a way to escape the troubles at home. While other men are experiencing career difficulties and disappointments and yet are able to compartmentalize these work problems, not allowing it to affect their ability to be *great* husbands.

Work is a place where men can focus their efforts, to be rewarded and praised for achievements which creates a sense of worthiness. They will take charge on the job, make things happen, solve problems and do what it takes to succeed. When there is trouble at home this same type of effort may not be displayed. Wives will say, "How can he be so successful, take the initiative, and be in charge at work, but at home he's passive, distant, checked out, or disengaged from the family?" The wife is frustrated and the husband may not have the emotional energy to really discuss the reasons why he truly has two different performance levels for home and work. What we ultimately want to strive for is what Zig Ziglar said many years ago, and that is to have a home court advantage. When a man feels accomplished, respected, and loved at home he can conquer the world 9 to 5 and then can't wait to get back home to be with his wife and family.

Work on Yourself

One of my favorite quotes about work comes from Jim Rohn: "Work harder on yourself than you do on your job. If you work hard on the job, you'll make a living. If you work hard on yourself you'll make a fortune." Many of you reading this book are no doubt hard workers on your job and give your employer your best efforts, talents, and mental focus. I'm not sure many of you are working just as hard or even harder on yourself. When you work harder on yourself, it will propel you in your career, because you'll be more valuable to your employer. More importantly, it will propel you as a man, as a husband to your wife, and father to your children. Working hard on yourself means seeing the areas that need to be improved and addressing them sooner than later, as you are intentional about your growth and career goals.

I have also heard personal development guru, Brian Tracy, say that "80% of people in the workforce are no better off today in their jobs then they were after the first year of that employment." He makes the case that comfort and complacency get in the way of people pursuing career advancement to their fullest potential. So I encourage you keep striving for improvement and development when it comes to your professional life. Don't be part of the 80% that are just doing enough to stay employed. Instead, work hard to be in the 20% that are advancing in their careers.

Furthermore, establishing a mentor in your career can accelerate your progress and refine your abilities. Some companies connect employees with mentors so take advantage of that system. If no such company policy exists, then you'll need to secure one on your own. The mentor relationship is one where you will have to identify the mentor, be willing to be held accountable by them and willing to maintain the relationship. The best mentor-mentee relationships exist because the mentee takes personal responsibility to ensure they meet regularly. If you can succeed in your professional life, you can also succeed in your life as a husband.

Avoiding Destructive Emotions

When we are not working on our own career, professional life, and subsequently income-producing activities, it is easy to succumb to destructive feelings. Thoughts and feelings of envy, jealousy, and inferiority, can creep into our conscious awareness as we see other men accomplishing great things in their professional lives. Although men don't like to confess it, we too can struggle with these destructive emotions.

So I encourage you to work on your own professional development and maximize every gift and talent that you have, so that you'll be in a place of fulfillment and peace. By doing this, you will keep these destructive emotions in check, and you will be comfortable celebrating the contributions of other men around you. It will also keep burnout and disgruntled feelings at a distance. Subsequently, the higher you advance in your career the more you will be able to provide for your wife and children.

On the other hand, never pursue advancement in your career at the expense of your relationship with your wife. Learning to balance your ambitions with the priority of keeping a strong healthy relationship with your wife is a lifelong process. I implore you to continue acquiring the skills in your chosen profession and participate in continuing education in order to add value as an employee and as a husband.

Overcoming Work Frustrations

We should also be proud of an honest day's work, regardless of our profession as a blue-collar or white-collar worker. Every day, work hard and smart for your employer. Give them a day's work for a day's pay. If you're the boss, then treat your employees fairly and pay them appropriately. In both instances, honesty on the job can translate into honesty at home with your wife.

As the leader of *Team Family*, there are certain roadblocks that can hinder us from putting in an honest day's work. Common ones include, when we don't feel valued and appreciated, and believe we have been overlooked for a promotion. When these things occur in the workplace, it can create anger, bitterness and resentment. It is incredibly difficult to give our employer our best with these cancerous emotions inside of us.

You may be completely justified feeling the way you do, so I'm not asking you to deny or bury those emotions. What I am saying is that being able to process them appropriately and keeping the right perspective while still employed is the right thing to do. It may not be economically feasible for you to just quit your job because of all that you've been through, since you have a wife and family. I believe some of the best ways to still do your job with these conflicting emotions and play in the paint like the big men is to:

i) Be thankful that you have a job that enables you to pay your bills and provide for your family. Gratitude with help to lessen the intensity of the emotions and allow to you still be present on the job and get your work done;

ii) Come to grips with your reality. Your employer is who they are and chances are they are probably not going to change. So readjusting how you perceive their actions or inactions will help you focus and see the situation realistically. Realizing that you won't be one of the favorites, or won't be the one given opportunities helps to lessen your disappointment because you are clear about where you stand on the totem pole; and

iii) Talk with your wife extensively about the issue and begin strategizing with her about when and how you will resign from that position and move on to where you can maximize your talents and attributes. This third piece is critical for a number of reasons: when you come home frustrated and irritated, then your wife won't take it personally because she'll understand the pressures and complexities on your job. She will be able to pray for you and that your situation will improve. By talking with her about your career decisions, she will feel that you value her wisdom and insight, which will increase her love and connection to you.

No one wants to be in a bad work situation, but stay positive with a belief that you are not stuck there forever. This is a temporary phase. Working with your wife to improve this situation will lessen your fear of change and give you the strength and support to transition when the time is right.

Points in the Paint

1. **Purpose**: Fulfill your purpose and calling in life to maximize all the gifts and talents that have been bestowed upon you. This gives your life rich meaning and provides an example for your wife to follow. It also leaves an inheritance for her and your future generations.

2. **Team Family**: Keep family time boundaries as sacred as possible. If you have on your calendar that Friday night is family time then stick to it. When people ask if you're available that night simply tell them "No," that you have a prior commitment.

3. **Respect**: Treat all the women on your job as you would your mother or sister to ensure that you never cross any boundaries of infidelity or sexual harassment.

4. **Prioritize**: Your job is not your life. It is something you do to earn a living for your family. Your life is found outside of work with your family and in the things that give you meaning and purpose. If you make work your "everything" then if work becomes an unbearable

place to be, your world becomes miserable.

5. **Presence**: When you leave work, process everything that occurred emotionally and psychologically on your commute home, so that when you walk through your front door your mind is fully present with your wife.

6. **Footprint**: Pick a problem on your job and create a solution that is sustainable. If the solution only works because you're employed there, then it is unsustainable. This means after the problem has been fixed, train others who can ensure that it remains solved after you're gone.

7. **Reputation/Integrity**: Whether you've just been hired or worked at the company for 10 years, make the determination that the company and its employees will be better because you've been employed there. Leave your position in a better place than you've found it.

8 **Advancement**: Don't keep your wife in the dark about your job and career. When you come home and she asks how was work, don't give the patent three word response, "it was fine." She may not need to know every detail, but debriefing with her just a little bit, may help you decompress and will make her feel more connected to you.

9. **Plan /Diligence**: If you are laid off or fired, it's not the end of the world. Be diligent in seeking another job as soon as possible. If you cannot find work within a reasonable amount of time then collect unemployment if you have to, but keep in mind that it is temporary. Of

course, it is discouraging to not find a job in your profession, however do not become lazy and sit at home and do nothing. Working anywhere to earn income to provide for your family is always better than not working at all.

CHAPTER 7

SHOW ME THE MONEY

"Wide Receivers only want to talk about two things, themselves and their money".
- **Cris Carter, Pro Football Hall of Famer**

Today, professional athletes make an enormous amount of money. We see their salaries and signing bonuses with guaranteed money whether or not they play a season. What we don't see, are the years of hard work on the practice field, in the weight room, and the countless hours of film study sessions. We don't witness the missed family gatherings, birthdays, holidays, declined events, or down time with close friends. They were focused on staying on track to accomplish their dream of becoming a professional athlete. After years of hard work, physical pain, and successful game-time performances, they finally get to reap the fruits of their labor with incredible salaries that the average working American cannot fathom.

Money and Marriage

Money is one of the main causes of disagreement in a marriage. These disagreements can become so intense that it ultimately leads to divorce for many couples. There are a variety of reasons couples find themselves in conflict with one another when it comes to the finances. More often than not the husband and wife have different perspectives when it comes to the meaning, value, and use of money. Some see money as a safety and security, and they want a certain amount of money to remain in the bank and need every bill paid on time. While others view money as the means to enjoy life, because you only live once on this earth. They know the bills have to be paid and things have to get done, but they refuse to live like a pauper. Inevitably, one spouse is usually the saver in the family while the other is more of a spender. One can manage the finances well and is consistent and disciplined to ensure all of bills are paid while the other spouse may not share these same attributes and qualities. The task for every married couple is to work through these differences so that they are on the same team when it comes to the finances.

Every great team is comprised of players with various talents and abilities to help the team win. The same is true with you and your wife as it relates to money. Each of you has to personally come to terms with what strengths you bring to the table and own the weaknesses that have caused failure in the past. Then as the husband, as the leader of the team, it is our responsibility to put our wife and our self in the financial roles that will move the team forward. For instance, if you aren't good with budgeting but she is then allow her to do the monthly budget while you stay informed and engaged in the process. It doesn't really matter who does what financial task, what matters is that the task you're both entrusted with is what you and your wife can do consistently well.

We can spend so much time fighting the weaknesses rather than maximizing the strengths of each other. In fact the differences that you share should not be fought over but used to help the team improve. The saver in the family needs the spender because without the spender the family won't enjoy life to the fullest. The spender in the family needs the saver because without the saver the family won't have the necessary resources now and in the future to live comfortably.

Money and Manhood

When a husband has the money necessary to take care of his wife and family it increases his personal esteem and strengthens his self-image. A husband feels like a man when he can provide for his family. We also know that when a husband lacks the necessary money it can take a toll on his pride and ego. The lack of resources due to poor money management or low wage scale challenges our masculinity. For many men their sense of being successful is directly tied to their bank account and ability to address the financial needs of the family.

I remember years ago when limited financial resources affected my sense of worth as a husband. My wife and I were in the process of selling our first home to purchase a larger home after the birth of our son. We saw numerous types of homes in the area we wanted to live; single family, duplexes, townhouses, and the traditional handy-man specials. Although we had a real estate agent, we also scanned our favorite neighborhoods for homes that were "For Sale by Owner".

One day while driving throughout a particular neighborhood we spotted what we thought was our dream home. It was older home that needed a lot of renovations. It was located within a cul-de-sac and had a nice portion of land connected to it. My wife and I made an appointment with the homeowner to tour the home.

When we arrived, there was an elderly gentleman trying unsuccessfully, to renovate the home. He was friendly and graciously gave us a tour of the house. It needed a lot of work; new kitchen, new bathrooms, carpet, walls, windows, roofing—you name it. We decided to place an offer on the home and told the man that we would come back the next day with a written offer based on the value of the home and in light of all of the work that needed to be done. He agreed that was fair and looked forward to seeing us the next day.

We raced home and carefully calculated what the repairs would cost and what the value of the home might be considering its condition. The more we thought about the home and its potential, the more we wanted it. We even thought that perhaps there would be some divine intervention for us when we made the deal because the owners had placed wooden heart shaped pieces on the garage door—remember my last name is Hart. The following morning, my wife, my five-month-old son and I got to the home to make our offer. The homeowner and his wife allowed us to present our offer in the kitchen. He took one look at the offer and in anger and disgust said, "That's an insult to me and my wife. This conversation is over, you can leave now." We tried to plead our case as to why we offered what we did but he wouldn't hear any of it.

I wasn't making a lot of money then and neither was my wife. We gave them our best offer based on what we could afford which wasn't much. The truth is also that the home was overpriced and we were trying to get it at a more reasonable price. Rather than treating us with dignity and respect and take into consideration that we were a young couple with a new child, they treated us like insignificant people who didn't belong in their presence. Defeated and demoralized we picked up our belongings and our son and made our way to the car.

It was raining so I held the umbrella over all of us, and as we walked to the car my wife began to cry. Once again, we weren't able to get the house we wanted because we didn't make enough money. This feeling of rejection happened a lot during our home buying process. I didn't blame my wife; her tears cut me to the core of my masculinity. As the man, as the husband, I didn't have the financial resources to provide for my family. It was on that day that I made a committed decision to work as hard as I could to earn as much as I could to provide for my family. I was committed to having the finances we needed so that my wife would never have to cry again because we didn't have the resources for our basic necessities.

Truthfully, I didn't have the financial resources because I wasn't pursuing career advancement to the best of my ability.

I will never forget that experience and it still drives me today to maximize all of my gifts, talents, and imagination to provide for my family. I share my story because it illustrates the point that our financial life significantly affects our self-image as a man and a husband. Money doesn't define you as a man, nor as a husband. It is your character and integrity and how you care for your loved ones that define you as a man and husband. Money will come and go, it's our character that helps us endure tough financial times and keep prosperity in perspective when it arrives. However your bank account and income does speak to whether or not you have maximized all of your earning potential. You have more than enough inside of you to provide for your wife and family because you've been given talents and abilities from a God who carefully crafted you. Your answers to financial increase first start with what is inside of you or as a friend of mine says, what's already in your hand. The more we maximize all of our abilities the more our esteem, sense of worth and significance as a man and husband increases even when the money hasn't yet arrived into our account.

When we pursue our purpose our life will revolve around making a difference in the lives of others and not in the accumulation of money. Money is not the root of all evil. It's the *love* of money that is the root of all evil. There is nothing wrong with having and making money. We just have to be sure that we own the money and it doesn't own us. The penalty flag to this is that we must be careful not to allow the love of money to rule and own us. When we love money more than being significant in this earth our perception of success will be distorted and unhealthy.

Financial Fundamentals

Every great athlete has mastered the fundamentals of their position to success game in and game out. There are also some financial fundamentals that we as husbands need to master as well. Our ability to have solid financial fundamentals will allow us to save, manage, and invest the money we earn in our lifetime. Furthermore, it is our responsibility to ensure our wife and children learn these same fundamentals. Let me be clear though, I am a marriage counselor, not a financial advisor. Therefore, I am going to give you some fundamentals as it relates to finances. These suggestions are based on what I often see missing in the lives of husbands who come for marriage counseling. If you have these points addressed, than I strongly suggest you sit down with your accountant and/or financial advisor and begin building off of what you have already. I also strongly recommend you take full advantage of the work done by Dave Ramsey and his Financial Peace University courses and the Legacy Series they offer as well. The teaching of Dave Ramsey has changed the trajectory of my financial life and I believe it will do the same for you. With that being said, below are four suggestions to get you started on the road to financial freedom.

1) Create a Monthly Budget

The most fundamental financial skill is creating and maintaining a monthly budget. The budget determines how money is spent, saved, invested, and donated. It provides a game plan for every dollar that comes into your possession each month. It is far more effective for the budget to be completed before the actual month begins. Furthermore, it is even more advantageous when the budget is completed for three to six months in advance. This allows to us not only address the present but also be mindful of what's coming down the road. When we budget month to month it's sometimes hard to have a long term perspective.

The budgeting process is a skill that can be learned but then it becomes a disciplined way of living. The skill can be learned in an afternoon but it may take much longer for it to become a discipline. This is usually where the conflict between spouses begins, when the budget is completed inconsistently in the home. Couples also have differing opinions as to what should and should not be on the budget, how it should actually look, and which systems to employ. If you and your wife have found yourselves with these differing opinions than you're in good company because many couples have this struggle initially. Once you both are on the same page and have agreed upon the right system life can get easier.

Where I see the most conflict though with the budgeting process is that the husband is not engaged in the process. He has taken a passive approach to this task leaving it for his wife to fulfill. The entire burden of the day to day financial management of the family should not fall solely on the shoulders of the wife. If you've been disengaged then become engaged again. You can't come in with the attitude that you're going to take everything over because that will create even more strife. A better approach is to learn the system already in place and get caught up to speed with what the financial picture looks like. Over time, you'll be able to offer your input, take on tasks, and you may end up doing the budget yourself.

Additionally, being in total control of the finances and leaving your wife in the dark is also problematic. She needs to know what is in the account, what the bills are, how things get paid, what the passcodes are, and when things are due. She should be able to open your financial planner or binder and know where to find things. Shielding her from this knowledge is actually very detrimental to her in the long run. I've seen husbands keep their wife in the dark and when he died the wife had no clue how to pay the bills, when things were due or even how to access the accounts online.

The goal of budgeting is for both the husband and wife to be agreement for the how the money will be spent and how that occurs. The more accurate and consistent the budget is the greater your financial success will become.

2) Get out of Debt

Unfortunately the average couple is in debt and owes thousands of dollars from consumer debt, student loans, and mortgage payments to name a few. Debt creates stress and pressure on the family and it delays their wealth building opportunities. Just think of what your life would be like if you had no debt. Perhaps that is too daunting of a task, because the debt is so high. So what if everything was paid off except your mortgage? Even if your salary hadn't increased but your debt was eliminated your life would be much easier. You would probably have less conflicts with your wife about money since you would have what you need to live with extra left over.

I offer that scenario as a way to motivate you to stop using credit cards to pay for things, start using cash only, and begin paying off your debt as quickly as possible. For many the process of getting out of debt is two-fold. First we have to believe we can actually get of debt regardless of how much we owe. We have to believe it is possible. If we don't believe it's possible we'll never try in the first place. Second we have to change the way we live now so that the day of being debt free becomes a reality. Our perception and thoughts about debt has to change to the point where we dislike owing other people. The budget is so important for it gives you the game plan for eliminating debt and using cash to pay for things. We also have to be willing to say "no" to a lot of things and activities initially. There is a period of sacrifice and denial that takes place when we are getting out of debt. But if we say no longer enough to debt eventually we get to say yes to so many things we have put on hold.

Sometimes one spouse is ready to eliminate debt and the other is not as enthusiastic. As the husband if you are ready and your wife isn't then I offer a few coaching points. Take it slow at first, making dramatic changes with the money will cause her to fight the debt elimination process even more. Share with her what life could be like if you didn't have any debt payments and ask her how she thinks life would be different. When we have an agreed upon picture of what life can and will look like one day we can work together to achieve it. You'll also have to make some adjustments and changes along the debt elimination journey. Sometimes you'll have to spend money when you wanted to use it for something else. That is part of the journey together and when we compromise with her it will make it easier for her to compromise with us later one.

If you have been the one resistant to getting out of debt I strongly encourage you to change your mind on the subject. Your wife is waiting for you to get on abroad with the process and once you do your life will see changes for the better. When a resistant husband joins his wife who is committed to debt elimination the process rapidly advances. It will initially be hard for you with the change in spending habits but you'll adjust sooner than you think. The adjustments will make you stronger individually and as a couple.

Becoming and living debt free is possible, every day another couple is paying off a bill and getting out of debt. My wife and I are on that journey with you as I write this book. I too am working and believing to make being debt free a reality for our household. Getting out of debt is one the most important financial fundamentals we can acquire to be a *great* husband.

3) Plan for Retirement

Planning for retirement is something many postpone only to regret later in life. When we are in our 20's and 30's retirement seems so far away but it approaches faster than we can imagine. There are a variety of ways to plan for retirement from 401K plan, IRA's, and ROTH IRA's. There isn't a shortage of retirement plans and strategies for us to choose. If your company offers a retirement plan than participate as much as you possibly can with your income going into those accounts. If your company doesn't offer it there are plenty of organizations that specialize in this financial goal.

I'm sure you and your wife want to live in dignity, pleasure, and without financial worries when the working days are over. The only way to ensure that happens is to plan for the day when you will no longer be employed full time. It does mean we make some sacrifices now but the power of compound interest in our retirement accounts will make the sacrifices worth it. Lastly, I'd say that unfortunately, working as a Pastor we often see a husband pass away and he didn't have a retirement savings account to leave for his wife and children. A measure of greatness as a husband is what you will leave for your wife and children as an inheritance for them when you are gone.[9]

4) Life & Disability Insurance

A frightening reality is that many couples do not have life insurance. A key to being a *great* husband is being responsible and planning for the day of your demise. Life insurance allows you to take care of your family when you are gone. The younger and healthier you are the cheaper it will be for you to acquire. Just like retirement planning, there are several life insurance companies that you select. Sometimes men will tell me that they have life insurance but it's with their employer. As great as that is, it's probably not enough. Furthermore, what happens if you lose that job than what coverage do you have while you secure employment. We need our own life insurance policies in addition to what any employer offers.

In terms of disability insurance, this is probably the one that most husbands do not have today. Disability insurance helps you to pay for your monthly expenses when you can no longer work full time due a disability that you have suffered. When husbands do have this, it is through their employer. Rarely though do I meet a husband who has his own disability insurance. If your present income has prevented you from obtaining disability insurance than work your budget to the point where that can be a line item for you. Perhaps when one of your consumer debts are paid off that will free up the money to get adequate disability insurance. Protect your family and yourself with the right amount of life and disability insurance.

Safety Points

1. **Teamwork**: Once you are married, it is no longer "your" money and "her" money, it now becomes "our" money. It's ok for each of you to have a personal account, but those accounts should be funded from a joint account that both of your salaries are deposited where all of the bills and expenses are addressed first.
2. **Cooperation**: Fighting about money with your wife never brings more money into you house or helps you to manage the funds you currently have. Cooperate with each other so that you can work together to bring in the resources your family needs.
3. **Sharing**: Take turns doing the finances so that both

parties are involved.

4. **Learning**: Attend financial planning seminars at least once a year to learn how to live debt-free and make your earnings work for you. I have completed Dave Ramsey's Financial Peace University classes and highly recommend them.

5. **Appreciation**: When your finances permit, hire a chef and a maid to give your wife a break from cooking and cleaning at least one day a month.

6. **Quality Time**: Plan a vacation with your wife only at least once a year and a family vacation with the kids at least once a year.

7. **Giving Back**: Designate a portion of your income to donate to charity. In the Christian faith, there is something called tithing, where people give 10% of their income to the church. Donating our funds to worthy organizations or causes keeps us from becoming greedy and tight with our money.

CHAPTER 8

Heart & Soul to Win

"I'm going to play with every inch of me on this field! Every ounce of my blessing! Every ounce of what I've got! It's going to be laid out!

-**Brian Dawkins**

The athletes that fans love the most are the ones who put their heart and soul into every game, and into every play. These athletes play with a passion and enthusiasm that is contagious. They are the guys who are in the middle of the team before the game starts, getting everyone fired up. They are so on fire that even as we watch the pre-game show, we get goosebumps just hearing them through the television. They arouse our soul and awaken our passion for the game so much so we think about skipping the game altogether and going outside to play the sport ourselves.

Brian Dawkins was that player on the Philadelphia Eagles

who would inspire and motivate the entire team. For years, he was the heart and soul of the defense and many would agree, the team as well. As passionate as he was on the field, he carried that same intensity in his relationship with God. When his career was over, he was known as both a great safety and a Godly man off the field.

However, Dawkins' story throughout his time in the NFL wasn't always one to be admired. Brian has been open to the fact that in his first year in the NFL he contemplated suicide. He was having marital problems, money problems, and started drinking more. He readily admits that it was nothing on the field that turned his life around. His life changed dramatically when he gave his life over to God and started to mature and grow in his spiritual life.

Spirituality

I believe one of the necessary ingredients to being a *great* husband is to have heart and soul. Not just a heart and soul for your wife, but more importantly, to have heart and soul for your spiritual development; to be passionate and enthusiastic about your spiritual growth. I truly believe that we are comprised of three parts: mind, body, and spirit. Just like we have to feed our mind and body to work properly, we also have to feed our spirit. Some people use the term soul instead of spirit, but the meaning is still the same. As men, our spiritual life is probably the most neglected aspect our lives and at the same time, one of the most important. Growing spiritually is an important component to becoming a *great* husband.

Before we move further, I want to draw a distinction between spirituality and religion. Religion can be defined as the *external* expression of a set of doctrines, rituals, and worship experiences that usually have some type of denominational underpinnings. Spirituality, however, can be defined as the *internal* expression of beliefs, values, needs, and desires, that connect to a person's sense of purpose and meaning as it relates to a Higher Power. Some people are religious, but don't necessarily consider themselves spiritual, while others identify themselves as spiritual and not religious. Then, there are those men whose religion and spirituality is intertwined, so that one influences the other.

I believe every single person has a spirit. Subsequently, since we have a spirit as part of our makeup as human beings, we all then have a spiritual life. Therefore, it's essential to find spiritual nourishment for our spirit just as regularly as we find physical nourishment for our physical bodies. For some men, their spiritual life is well defined and understood because of the teachings of their particular religion. For others, their spiritual life is loosely defined and seems to be a work in progress. There are also those who do not subscribe to the idea that we all have a spirit at all. For the purposes of this book, your spiritual life can be defined as the beliefs *you* have about a Divine existence. These beliefs serve as the foundation for the values you live by that give you a sense of purpose and meaning. Those values guide your decisions as an individual, with your family, community and society as a whole.

Comfort Zones

For men that are firmly rooted with a sense of spirituality, their beliefs and actions as a husband flow effortlessly to incorporate the spiritual disciplines into their marriage. For many other men that I speak with and counsel, their spirituality is out of their comfort zone when compared to their professional, financial, and personal life. I often hear men say that they find it difficult to become spiritual leaders in the home because their wife is more "spiritual" than they are. Their wives regularly attend religious services or religious activities. She is embracing her spirituality more often by praying and reading sacred texts. I realize that men have legitimate apprehensions or concerns about their spirituality, so I recommend practicing these three action steps to improve your spiritual journey.

The first step starts with coming to a conclusion about what you believe and value. You must be firmly convinced in your beliefs to lay the foundation that you'll build upon. Without clarity, you'll continue to wander aimlessly through this life in search of spirituality. Your wife won't follow you spiritually if you if you are unsure of where you are going.

The second step that's needed is consistently participating in scheduled devotional time or spiritual disciplines. The term devotional or spiritual disciplines is a catch all phrase to describe the various activities that you can participate in, to have a vibrant, healthy spiritual life. This can include: prayer, meditation, reading sacred texts, moments of silence and contemplation. Carving out this consistent time is often a challenge for men, since we are driven by action, movement, activity, and accomplishment. All of this doesn't lend itself well to times of quiet, thoughtful prayer, reading, and contemplation.

Many of us feel as though we are running 24/7 to accomplish all that is set before us. When we look at our responsibilities to our family, our job, and our interests, there never appears enough time to juggle them all. Men mistakenly believe that they can endure long periods of time in between their devotional experiences. In fact, this doesn't appear to be a 21st century problem for men. Hundreds of years ago French scientist and philosopher Blaise Pascal observed, "I have discovered that all the unhappiness of men arises from one single fact: that they cannot stay quietly in their own chamber." The success of your spiritual life will be directly connected to your ability to consistently have devotional time.

Additionally, we have a great role model to follow as we develop our spirituality. I find encouragement and perspective from Jesus who often withdrew from his disciples to pray, to be renewed, and to seek guidance. No one was busier than Jesus as he traveled preaching the good news and raising a generation of disciples to lead His cause after His predetermined death on the cross. I often say to myself, *if Jesus made devotional time an important act of obedience, then I have no excuses.*

The third step to improve your spiritual life is to take action. There are two scripture verses that speak to this, "don't just hear the word, but put it into practice," [10] and "faith without works is dead."[11] It's easier to believe in spiritual principles than it is to practice them. Yet, with more practice, we grow and mature. This will reveal aspects of our life that needs to be improved, habits we need to relinquish, and attitudes that must be changed.

The more committed we are to spiritual growth, the more it will require of us to change for the better. The spiritual values we choose to live by will always call for us to live a higher, more sacrificial way of living:

When our spiritual values call for forgiveness,
we need to forgive.

When they call for maturity, we must be mature.

When they call for humility, we must be humble.

When they call for us to love our wife, we must love her unconditionally.

When they call for patience, grace, and respect,
we must respond.

When they call for tenderness and love,
we must act accordingly.

When they call on us to be courageous,
we must take a stand to protect.

We must not disengage or withdraw from these spiritual calls to action, but face them head on. I advise you to embrace your beliefs and values, participate in spiritual disciplines, and act upon the Word as a doer and not just a hearer. If you implement these three action steps, your initial concerns about a lack of spirituality will disappear and your spiritual growth will begin to accelerate at a steady pace.

Bringing Your Spirituality Home

When you begin your spiritual life walk, your wife will appreciate it. Wives welcome the spiritual initiatives of their husbands regardless if he hasn't been spiritual up to this point in their marriage. Women appreciate spirituality and the sense of connectedness that it brings to them and their relationship with their husband. However, a word of caution: If you decide after reading this book to believe in a particular religion and your wife doesn't subscribe to that belief then walk very slowly and carefully when initiating spiritual activities. I'm not saying don't share your new found faith, what I am saying is that no one likes to have a belief shoved down their throat.

If your spiritual life is different than your wife's, respect her belief system and initiate spiritual activities that you both can agree upon that will be mutually beneficial. One day she may share the spiritual life that you've embraced, but until then make the goal spiritual connection rather than spiritual agreement.

If you decide to join in the spiritual life that your wife already embraces, know that she has been longing for you to join her. When you start following these spiritual life strategies, her heart will sing and she will feel even more secure and further connected to you than ever before. Grow at a steady pace and don't feel pressured to immediately meet all of your wife's expectations in this area.

I would also encourage you that if you have not been

practicing your beliefs in a while, don't allow the thoughts of hypocrisy to ruin your desire to have a spiritual life. There is the dynamic that the more spiritual your wife is the more important it will be on her list of needs and wants as a wife and in her marriage. The more important it will be for her that her husband is spiritual and practices the spiritual disciplines regularly. When you realize that and move in the direction of prayer and devotional time for our own growth she will admire and respect your commitment. Even when wives aren't that spiritual, they still appreciate and find comfort in a husband who is spiritual and connected to the divine.

The Power of Two

In addition to your own personal spiritual disciplines, there is also the importance and power of engaging in spiritual practices with your wife. The scripture tells us that in regards to prayer, one person can put 1,000 angels into action, whereas if two people touch, agree, and pray they can put 10,000 angels into action.[12] Talk about the power of two! However, many Christian men who know this verse fail to implement it in their own homes on a regular basis. As I've mentioned before, if a man feels insecure or inadequate in this area he'll be less willing to engage in these actions. Yet most wives long for the days when their husbands are spiritual leaders in the home, taking the initiative to pray, reading sacred texts, and having family devotional time. These practices bring security to a wife, and peace to a home.

Don't be afraid to take the initiative and pray with your wife regularly. Don't allow your own failures and moral shortcomings to perpetuate guilt and remorse. We all have failed, and many more times than just once. Remember the story of Adam in the Garden of Eden. He had everything at his disposal, no financial pressures, a beautiful wife, great place to live, secure and stable income, a personal tangible relationship with God. He had it all, and yet he still failed by eating of the tree of the knowledge of good and evil. If Adam had it all and still screwed up, guess what, we'll make mistakes too and fall short of our moral expectations. But don't stay there, confess and repent of your sins and move forward with God. Use the spiritual disciplines you acquired for yourself, and use them with your wife.

It will take planning and timing to have these spiritual experiences with your wife regularly but we can do it. And I want to stress the word, regularly; it doesn't have to mean every morning, every afternoon, or every evening you're in prayer with your wife. Regularly means you consider your schedules, your daily and weekly activities and decide when are the best times each week to practice spiritual disciplines with your wife. For some men they can do it every morning, for some families the evenings are better, still for others it's on an every other day basis. While others do it just once a week. Whatever the regular schedule is for your family keep to it and keep it realistic. If you haven't done any spiritual disciplines with your wife in 6 months, it may be unrealistic to think you're going to do it now every morning and evening. Be realistic and be consistent and the growth will come in time.

Furthermore don't foolishly believe you can grow spiritually as an individual, a couple, or a family in isolation. As the husband, it is your responsibility to ensure that you, your wife and children, are consistent and active members of a religious community (ie: church, synagogue, etc). We need the power, support, wisdom, strength, and guidance of a community of believers to help us as men, as husbands, and as a family. The community has so much to offer you and you in turn have so much to offer the community. Don't get discouraged, there is a religious community for everyone. If you haven't found the one that fits you and your family, keep looking, you are bound to find it.

Don't fall prey to the excuses that everyone in the church is a hypocrite or all they want is my money, or the service is too loud, too long, too short, or I have softball games on Sunday, or it's guys time on Sunday morning. Men can come up with so many excuses for not going to the religious community. Don't let "Mr. Excuses" be you. If you want to be a *great* husband, you'll put an end to all of the excuses that hinder your personal, couple, and family spiritual growth.

Where I Stand

By now, you fully realize that I identify as a Christian, so my relationship with Jesus Christ and the Bible influences and directs my spiritual life. If you're already a Christian, I hope this book will motivate you to further improve your relationship with Christ. At the same time, I recognize the challenge of creating strategies for husbands to live by in the area of their spiritual life when there are so many different belief systems that men can subscribe too.

I teach a course at Rutgers University called *Spirituality in Social Work*. It covers the major religions and as we review these different belief systems, it is clear that there are some common themes that are addressed by all of them. The majority of these themes include the meaning of life, hope, suffering, and the afterlife. The answers to those themes however, vary greatly. They use different sacred texts to guide their lives along with different ways of expressing their beliefs individually and corporately. I encourage you to live out the spiritual disciplines of your faith to help you become a great husband. For those you of who follow Christianity I too encourage you to live out your faith to the fullest in order to be a *great* husband to your wife. Every man needs to answer to a higher, authority to govern their actions and decisions. If the only person you ever answer to is yourself, you'll never reach your fullest potential as a husband.

Scoring Points

1. **Daily Devotion**: A personal daily devotional time to nurture your spirit with your Higher Power as you understand, is essential for your success as a husband.

2. **Spiritual Food**: Be continuously in tune with and feed your spirit's needs so that you can fulfill your own purpose and calling and avoid the destructive paths that lead to failure. If we are hungry for dinner, but eat a Snickers instead, we can't enjoy dinner because we've satisfied our appetite with the wrong food. Our spirit is the same way. Don't feast on deceptive yet fulfilling

candy, but rather eat at the table of your sacred texts.

3. **Spiritual Strength**: Resist the temptation to participate in activities that would weaken or destroy your spiritual life. Every day we have a choice between living our lives with moral integrity or succumbing to temptations that provide immediate relief, but leave lasting negative consequences.

4. **Spiritual Role**: Never relinquish your spiritual leadership to your wife. As the husband, you are to be the spiritual leader in your home. You lead your wife by first leading yourself in the areas of spirituality and faith.

5. **Unconditional Support**: Ensure that your wife has every opportunity to grow and develop in her own sense of spirituality and life purpose. We should appreciate her desire for private time to practice her own spiritual disciplines. We should never diminish her spiritual beliefs or hinder her from practicing them. Furthermore, we should encourage her participation in spiritual or religious communities if they are places where she can grow and blossom as a woman, wife, and mother.

6. **Fellowship**: Find a religious community that you, your wife and family, can be regularly and active members. We go to our lawyer for legal advice, our mechanic for auto advice, our accountant for financial advice, so it stands to reason that we should go a spiritual leader (ie: pastor, rabbi, etc.) for spiritual advice. We find this

spiritual advice by being part of the religious community and the services that are offered.

7. **Forward Facing**: Kill every excuse, negative and condemning thought that hinders your spiritual growth and development. Past sins will always remind you of your failures, but we are more than our shortcomings. Listening to these thoughts will box into your past rather than freeing you to live in the present moment.

8. **Continuous Growth**: Utilize the tools of podcasts, YouTube videos, CD's, DVD's, audio books, etc. to listen to people who inspire and encourage you in our spirituality. Find the men who are sharing messages that you can relate to and that challenge you to grow. Subscribe to email lists or newsletter lists of people who are providing great material to help you grow and mature. Most of these can be sent right to your inbox and show up on your phone. Consistent consummation of positive, life affirming, spiritual material strengthens our soul.

9. **Obey God's Voice**: When you sense a desire to read a sacred text, or prayer, or spend a few moments in thought take advantage of them as soon as possible. God is often trying to get our attention about something and the temptation is to just keep working, check our phones, put the TV on, and surf the Internet. When you sense moments to engage in spiritual practices, take full advantage of them.

HALFTIME

HALFTIME RECAP

1st Quarter:

Team Family: Family First. Nothing and no one is more important in your life than your role as a husband and father. Provide for your family in the manner that God intended and you will have more victories than you could ever imagine.

Greatness and You: Greatness takes time, practice, commitment and focus. Yet it is relative. There is still time to be the greatest husband *you* can be to your wife.

Game Changers: View your marriage realistically and not what you see on TV, in the movies, or what your parents did. There are so many different family dynamics today that you have to be willing to adapt your situation and your wife.

Staying Inbounds: Review the list of things that keep you inbounds like focus, unity and communication. Try to stay out of bounds as much as possible to avoid becoming selfish, lazy, not following through, or mishandling money.

2nd Quarter

Distractions & Difficulties: Be more aware of distractions that can cause problems in your marriage, like your health, children, work, money, and emotional intelligence. Difficulties may arise if you are married to women with various negative dispositions that will need to be addressed at the appropriate time.

Winning At Work: Of course work is important, but make sure there is a balance with family boundaries. Distance yourself from emotional connections to women at work.

Show Me The Money: Your manhood is not determined by the amount of money you make. If you are lacking in the money management area, take classes to learn how to manage and budget money. Research adequate life insurance and retirement plans.

Heart & Soul to Win: Victory is not for the faint-hearted or the one who is ready to throw in the towel after a loss or difficulty. It is important to have values and a belief system to give you direction, comfort, and strength to lead with more vigor and determination after experiencing a challenge or loss.

GREAT HUSBANDS GAMEDAY
Channel WGHG

Sports Anchor: We're back in the studio. I have Coach Jim Hart here today to talk about the impact of leading thousands of committed men on the field and on the court as they begin to put in the work towards becoming great husbands. He's the author of *The Great Husband's Playbook: Winning Plays for a Victorious Marriage*. Coach Hart, thanks for joining us this afternoon.

Coach Hart: It's a pleasure to be here.

Sports Anchor: Now tell us, what inspired you to look at the role of a husband in terms of a quarterback or team captain?

Coach Hart: Well, guys come to me all the time with questions on how to make their marriage work or ask for suggestions about being a good husband. So, as I was writing this book, it hit me that there is no position more crucial to team sports than the quarterback in football. Of course, there are other important positions like the goalie in hockey and the pitcher in baseball. Yet, there is no one person that can dictate the trajectory of a team's success better than the quarterback. As a marriage counselor, I believe that same type of leadership role applies to the husband as the head or leader of his family. The better a man is at leading his wife and children, the more happiness and success they will have as a team.

Sports Anchor: I hear you on that point, but being a quarterback puts a lot of pressure on one person.

Coach Hart: I agree. It's both a fortunate and unfortunate position to be in. When the team is winning, you get all of the accolades. But when things aren't going well, you are the primary target to blame. I also see an issue with quarterbacks receiving too much self-credit, when it is truly a team effort to keep him out of harm's way to do his job effectively. If a husband is doing his job in the home, his wife and children will compliment his efforts and the household will be happy and better off.

Sports Anchor: Let's talk about some of the characteristics that a great husband and a great quarterback need to have.

Coach Hart: The first thing both need to have is great vision. A quarterback needs to have peripheral vision to beat the defense before the pre-snap. He needs to see his receivers and options in real time. Similarly, once you are married, you should have a five year plan and 10 year plan for your family. From what I see, it's not that guys don't have a plan, they just get so focused on the daily grind trying to pay the bills and keep their heads on straight, it's hard to focus on the future. This great vision requires men to think about where they want to be years from now, not just financially, but spiritually and relationally. This has happened to me in my own marriage. When my son turned six, my wife mentioned to me that we needed to start thinking about what happens when he turns 16. She is always thinking about the future. At the time, I found myself thinking about my next day's workload. To make this work, guys need to take their heads out of the daily grind and sit down with their wives and plan for the future. If they don't, they are missing out on the bigger picture...

Sports Anchor: That's funny you say that because my wife is the same way!

Coach Hart: I believe you. Most women are gifted that way.

Sports Anchor: I totally agree with you on that point. Now getting back to the husband and quarterback as leaders, can you run down a few key leadership principles that great husbands should identify with in leading their families to victory?

Coach Hart: Yes, there are several. I already mentioned the need for great vision. Like a great quarterback, a great husband needs to put in extra work. A quarterback needs to be the first on the field and the last to go home. He should have watched more film than any other player. A great husband needs to rise early and plan his day and be the last one to go to bed to ensure the family's needs are met and that they are well-protected. Both men should be the first to sacrifice and the last to be rewarded. Another key leadership characteristic is that both men need to have short memories: a quarterback has to forget the interception he just threw and a husband needs to forget the last disagreement he had with his wife. They both must be willing to shake off their past mistakes and have confidence that they are doing the right thing and that the plan will work out in their favor.

Sports Anchor: Yes, I was thinking the same thing. Not only do you have to outwork everyone else, but you should also be one step ahead of things.

Coach Hart: That's correct. You also need to be accountable to your wife and the team. Leadership without accountability is dictatorship. If you lead your team with an attitude that I can say and do whatever I want, they will not follow you. A dictatorship in your marriage leads to divorce. Husbands have to answer to their wives and children, and ultimately to God for what they did or did not do when the opportunity arose. Some men tend to isolate themselves from others and shun input from others, which can only breed destruction in the long run. You cannot lone-wolf it.

Sports Anchor: But you also cannot be expected to know how to do everything.

Coach Hart: That's why men should be encouraged to know that this great husband thing is doable, because you don't have to know everything. You can take classes in finance if you are not good with managing money or the household budget. That's what I did. There is plenty of information and resources to get you the information you need, even if it has to do with uncomfortable subjects like sex, communication, or trust issues. They key is knowing that you need help in an area and making a decision to get it. I see more and more men in my sessions because of poor decision making. At the end of the day, you have to be true to yourself and know your own abilities—your strengths and weaknesses.

Sports Anchor: Thanks for joining us Coach Hart. We're out of time. Viewers can learn more about the Playbook at greathusbandsplaybook.com. As we are going to commercial, check out a few extra plays to help you along your path to greatness.

Show your wife love, respect, and appreciation at all times.

Daily plays to remember:

Communicating

Your wife has a strong desire to communicate with you in order to feel connected, heard, appreciated, valued, and loved. So always keep the lines of communication open. I've heard it said that the death of communication is the birthplace of resentment, so don't stop communicating.

Take the high road and apologize to initiate the reconciliation process.

Never say to your wife after she gets a new haircut, "You look like a boy." I know because I actually said that! Don't lie to her, just be ever mindful of her sense of esteem, beauty, and dignity.

Listening

Learn how to discern when you're wife just wants you to listen to her and not solve any problems for her. But also learn when she wants to you listen and help her solve problems.

Contrary to popular opinion we don't have a listening problem as men we have an attention problem. We listen (pay attention) to the things that are important to us. Be sure that your wife's statements and requests remain important to you.

Sex

Never force your wife to do something in bed that she doesn't feel comfortable doing.

If you are having sexual performance issues with your wife, get professional, medical help-do not suffer in silence.

Remember that romance for your wife is as important to her as sex is to you.

When you wife is pregnant sex is on her terms. When she isn't pregnant sex is usually on her terms anyway.

Pregnancy

To the best of your abilities don't deny your pregnant wife anything! Be careful not to dismiss postpartum depression. Get her help if she needs it. Show understanding, love, and tenderness-your wife's life and your child's life depend on it.

Children

Never come home from work and kiss your children first and your wife last.

Never scold your wife for an unkempt house or dinner not prepared when she's been home all with your young children.

Consistent date nights with your wife after you have children aren't optional, they are mandatory. They will provide nourishment to starving souls longing for intimacy and connection.

In order to have a consistent, healthy sex life with your wife, keep your newborn children and children of any age out of the bed at night.

The more often you get up in the middle of the night to tend to a crying baby, the happier your wife will be.

Do not violate or disregard the system and structure your wife has created to keep the house and the children's belongings in order.

Handling Pressure/Stress/Anger

When angry with your wife it is never acceptable to physically harm her or use profanity to express your emotions. No silent treatments. Be cognizant of words and actions that devalue her as a person, damage her self-esteem or sense of worth as a wife, and possibly mother.

If arguing in the car about your driving, pull over and let her drive to avoid tension throughout the day.

Special Days/Holidays

Don't allow Hallmark or a national calendar to dictate when you show appreciation to your wife. Consider making the third Sunday in September "Wife Appreciation Day" or pick any day that is important to you. Of course, you cannot forget her birthday, your wedding anniversary, or Mother's Day. Remembering these critical plays throughout the year will keep you winning with your wife.

THIRD
QUARTER

CHAPTER 9

SCORING IN THE BEDROOM

"Golf and sex are about the only things you can enjoy without being good at it."

-Jimmy Demaret

Every golfer knows that a bad day on the golf course is better than a good day at the office. No matter how bad we play, just the experience of being on the golf course, occasionally hitting a great shot and enjoying the company of friends is what makes the sport so enjoyable. Our technique can be flawed, our equipment may need to be updated and we may not be able to stay in the fairway off the tee. Despite these challenges we will leave the course that day anticipating the next golf outing. The game has that kind of power over the golfer. This power is further strengthened on those rounds when we are hitting the fairways, making our putts and the scorecard reflects our actual ability. In those moments golf is exhilarating, it's addictive, because we are playing to our potential and it just feels so good.

Sex and intimacy in marriage has many parallels to the game of golf. Even when we aren't very good at making love to our wife, we still enjoy the experience and can't wait for the next time. Our technique may be flawed and our stamina wasn't what we wanted it to be, but that doesn't damper our desire for the next sexual experience. In a way, many men would agree that bad sex is better than no sex at all. Conversely, just like golf, when we are performing at our best and we are satisfying our wife's needs in the bedroom, our desire for more sex and intimacy can grow at a ferocious rate. When we aren't playing well on the golf course we go get a professional lesson. When we are playing well we want to know even more about the game. The same is true with sex and intimacy, to improve or hone our skills we probably need to seek professional guidance. There's nothing like hitting a perfect shot in golf just like there's nothing like a deep, rich, satisfying sexual experience, both leaving us wanting more.

But let's also be honest with each other, sexual compatibility between a husband and wife doesn't come naturally to every couple. For some couples, sexual compatibility and intimacy has never been an issue. Both are comfortable and proficient in the bedroom and there is great chemistry. Other couples haven't been compatible since the honeymoon and it's an issue that affects their relationship in many ways. While other couples have some good and bad days, overall the intimacy is good, but they realize there is always room for improvement.

Being a *great* husband in terms of sex and intimacy means we'll need to address the various factors that can affect this area of marriage with our wife.

Male Ego & Society

Much has been written and spoken about the male ego when it comes to sex and intimacy. Every guy wants to be the stud that can make love for hours and totally please his wife. The problem is that we are all human with abilities and limitations. When our limitations cause us to fall short of the ego's ideal, we tend to feel less than a man. If that happens, many men choose another venue for their sexual gratification or become more self-focused. By doing so, they miss the mark concerning the needs of their wives. We must approach sex with a realistic mindset of our strengths and limitations, and not the unrealistic demands of our egos.

Unfortunately, men are celebrated in society for their sexual conquests and for being "great" in bed. If you watch any movie, read any men's magazine or book, the emphasis is on men being extremely potent. If there is sexual dysfunction or difficulty, the man is mocked and ridiculed. How did this happen? Did our male egos create the societal portrayal or did the societal portrayals enhance our egos? The truth is, men are affected psychologically, emotionally, and relationally by the ego and the societal portrayal. Men must remember that much of our foundational ideas and long standing thoughts about sex and intimacy come not from personal experiences but the "fantasy" worlds of movies, TV, magazines, porn, and the "locker room" talk. Men have often had the experience that what they watched on TV didn't become a reality in their own bedrooms with their wife.

Women are Different

Women are different than men when it comes to sex and intimacy. Their definitions of pleasure, good sex, and needs being met are often different than what their husbands would articulate. It's interesting that men appear to have the same viewpoints regarding sex, yet one woman's sexual viewpoint can be vastly different from another woman. What pleases one doesn't please the other, what one likes another dislikes, how free they feel sexually certainly differs as well. This is no secret for men, but this truth presents a challenge. Men have told me they went to a Men's Conference and tried a few things on their wives that the speaker suggested. Much to their dismay, their wives resoundingly rejected their newly discovered love-making techniques stating that it didn't do anything for them. Husbands need to remember that each woman is unique and that their wives needs are ever-changing when it comes to sex and intimacy. What turns your wife on now, may not be the same thing six months to a year from now, and most certainly ten years from now. It will be helpful to filter through this information from the lens of what your wife wants and needs when it comes to sexual intimacy. By now, if you don't have a Ph.D. in your wife, you should at least have an Associate's Degree.

Past Relationships

This is another area that shouldn't come as a surprise to anyone. Husbands and wives have a relationship history individually before they became a couple. Some people have a history that is extensive, perhaps even promiscuous, with multiple partners and a variety of sexual experiences. Others get married with no sexual partners or significant relationships so they are coming to the marriage with a "clean slate." Most people have had a few relationships with moderate amounts of sexual experiences. What is important here is the match of histories between a husband and a wife. Every possible combination of matches has its own pros and cons. So, rather than dragging out the scenarios, allow me to offer three points.

(1) It is crucial that both husband and wife accept and come to terms with their own past and their spouse's past history.

(2) If the past is causing problems in the present, make every effort to uncover the root of the difficulty and work through it together.

(3) Don't compare your present spouse to past partners. In most cases, it won't draw you closer together, but rather create unhealthy emotions and expectations that will undermine your sexual intimacy.

Issues of Abuse, Molestation or Rape

Abuse, molestation, and rape at any age, usually have serious and far-reaching effects on those who were the victims of such destructive behavior. It can distort the person's sense of sexuality and perception of sex and intimacy. I have often counseled with couples whose times of sexual intimacy had been affected by the past abuse and pain. The spouse who was abused may have difficulty engaging in the activity while their partner feels powerless to make things better.

The best thing that can happen is for the spouse who has been abused to get professional help. In order a married couple to fully experience the joys of a sexual union, the trauma of past abuse should be addressed in a therapeutic setting. Additionally, when a person has experienced this type of trauma the depths of the pain will often be brought to the surface when they are in a safe, supportive, committed relationship. Oftentimes the pain is buried until the conditions are right for healing to begin. So if your wife is the one who was abused in this way, honor those moments by being patient, understanding, and supportive through the therapeutic process.

The worst thing that can happen is for person who was the victim of abuse is to be blamed for the abuse occurring in the first place. I have seen husbands say insensitive things to their wives such as, "I can see why you got abused with an attitude like that." Blaming the person for the abuse only adds more shame to their experience and they will no longer see their spouse as a safe and supportive individual. Sometimes a husband won't blame the spouse as just described, instead he doesn't understand how deep the pain is and how complexed it can make sexual experiences.

Being dismissive of her internal pain or making statements like "I didn't abuse you" or "you have to get over it because it was so long ago" will prolong her healing process and put more pressure on her to deal with an important process quicker than she is capable. I can't emphasize the need for professional help, great amounts of patience, and the focus being on healing first and a mutually satisfying sexual relationship as second.

Pornography

One of the most destructive forces in marriages today is the issue of pornography, which leads to masturbation and infidelity. Pornography is *not* a harmless art form as society tends to infer. It degrades the people who participate in it and it warps the minds and hearts of the people who consume it. As husbands, when we consume porn we are lusting after other women and we are dishonoring the commitment we made to be faithful to our wives only. It will also create unrealistic expectations for us as well.

Porn is all about self-gratification. It does not instill an atmosphere nor the mindset to be focused on the needs of the other person. I have yet to counsel a married couple where the wife was totally fine with her husband consuming porn. Most women see it as form of marital infidelity. For many women, they are disgusted by the videos and images and it causes them to see their husband with that same level of disgust. Wives are less willing to have sex with their husbands when they know he has sexual images of other women in the forefront of his mind. A couple's sexual experiences are often hindered and harmed because of porn rather than helped.

Porn is also what is known as an arousal addiction. Meaning men don't want more of the same image or video. Every image or video leads to a desire for even more intense and explicit images and videos. Therefore, the more porn you consume, the more explicit and perverted your mind will become. Furthermore, consuming porn leads to masturbation. There isn't a man I have known or counseled that looked at porn and did not masturbate. The reason masturbation is harmful in your marriage is because it puts the focus on you and off of your wife. It makes it about your immediate pleasure, not about mutual love-making. Sexual experiences were designed to take place between two married people, not by one person with themselves. If you are having problems with pornography then I recommend an excellent resource, *Every Man's Battle* by Stephen Arterburn & Fred Stoeker. Additionally, there are *Every Man's Battle* workshops that you can attend as well. For more information, log on to www.newlife.com.

Infidelity

"The more people rationalize cheating, the more it becomes a culture of dishonesty. And that can become a vicious, downward cycle. Because suddenly, if everyone else is cheating, you feel a need to cheat, too."

-Stephen Covey

Unfortunately, the issue of infidelity is one that I have had to deal with more than any other issue, in marriage counseling sessions. Affairs don't happen in an instant, nor do we wake up one day and decide to cheat on our spouse. Affairs are built slowly over time with consistent, inappropriate words and actions, coupled with our thoughts being consumed with another person. This process is usually initiated when there are problems at home between a husband and wife. The problems don't have to be just sexual incompatibility, for I have worked with couples who had great sex, but affairs still took place. Sexual incompatibility may be one of the contributing factors, but there are usually issues with communication, trust, affection, intimacy, money, respect and affirmation. When these issues are in play, it sets the stage for the path to infidelity. Although both spouses have a role to play as to the problems in the marriage, when one of them commits adultery that person has to take full responsibility for their actions.

Once an affair has occurred, don't make the mistake many couples commit by not getting professional help. Couples can't solve their infidelity problems on their own. They need the assistance of a professional counselor who helps couples with this specific problem. The recovery process for infidelity is not a simple three session fix. It takes a lot of time and effort to restore trust, love, and sex within your marriage. If you as the husband committed the affair, you will need to take full responsibility for your actions. You will have to carry the pain that your wife is experiencing. This is often done by answering her questions honestly and answering them again and again as she works through the pain. It means being accountable in every area of your life where every moment of your day is accounted for as you check in with her. This isn't something that's done for years on end, but certainly in the initial months after the affair. In addition, you'll have to work on the issues within yourself that got you to the place of infidelity in the first place.

"Between lovers a little confession is a dangerous thing."
-Helen Rowland

There is some debate as to whether or not you should tell your wife about the affair that ended when she hasn't found out yet. Different situations may call for different responses. For instance, there are some who believe that if you had an affair early on in your marriage, and many years have passed, that you should take it to your grave and be your cross to bear. By telling her of an affair that happened so many years ago, the argument is that you will be relieving your guilt by dumping this incredibly painful confession onto her to now bear. Some experts say that the loving thing to do is not tell her and you bear that cross yourself.

Those who make this argument might also apply this same type of thinking to affairs that happened more recently that have come to an end without your wife's knowledge. Certainly there are other experts who vehemently disagree with these perspectives and believe that there needs to be total honesty if your marital relationship will truly succeed and thrive. These individuals would further argue that if you don't tell her and she finds out herself or from a third party, it will be much worse than if you had just told her yourself.

As a pastor, I would error on the side of honesty over taking it to your grave. However, I also know that there are so many different scenarios that don't apply to a blanket statement that may not work for every case. So allow me to offer these points for you to consider:

i) Listen to what your personal convictions are telling you. What is your heart and mind saying about confessing this unfaithfulness. We often know what the right thing to do is, but don't have the courage to actually do it;

ii) If you tell her, you must be able to live the consequences that follow. Your wife may very well leave you and take the children with her. In addition, she may not leave you, but choose to make your life miserable for the rest of your days;

iii) Seek a very trusted, wise person who you can explain your situation to and request their assistance to guide you through the process. Don't make any decision by yourself within your own mind, you will be deceived in the end, and

iv) Always keep the faith/hope that there is a possibility of forgiveness, reconciliation and restoration. Whatever the outcome, you have to be willing to live with it.

"I told my wife the truth. I told her I was seeing a psychiatrist. Then she told me the truth: that she was seeing a psychiatrist, two plumbers, and a bartender."
— ***Rodney Dangerfield***

Unfortunately wives can have an affair as well and men process infidelity differently than women do. It's more common for women to be able to forgive and work on saving their marriage than it is for men. When a man's wife has cheated on him, it can shatter his ego, break his heart, and plague his mind. Men question their manhood and masculinity because of their wives infidelity. Despite a broken heart, we can usually recover from it over time. However, many men struggle with this in their minds. We are visual creatures and cannot erase the pictures of the sexual experiences another man engaged in with our wives.

Countless men have told me, "I just can't get the image out of my mind." Further, just as women have to learn to trust again, so do we as men. If you're in this situation, I would suggest you find out the basic facts, who, what, and when, but I caution you not to press her for every intimate detail. Seek help for yourself to work through the pain to determine if you want to stay in the marriage. You'll also need to take inventory as to where you may have contributed to any unhappiness in the marriage. The person who was cheated on isn't to blame for the affair, but they need to honestly look at what they did and did not bring to the table for their spouse. Recovery and restoration is possible, so if that is what you desire to occur, there are tons of couples who have overcome this hurdle, and you and your wife can as well.

Children Change Everything

Nothing throws a curveball into our sexual experiences with our wife like the birth and raising of children. When they are newborns, our patterns of living are disrupted and changed. More importantly, it can change how a wife perceives herself sexually. Before children, she was a wife, focused on your emotional and sexual needs. After children, she became a mom, focused on every aspect of their lives. Sex may not be a priority for her when the children are young. Furthermore, her body is going through hormonal changes, and if she is breastfeeding, she may be physically exhausted not to mention possibly sore from the experience. The last thing she may want is for you touch or kiss her breasts.

As the children get older, the physical demands of caring for a newborn are now spent chasing around toddlers. This changes to middle-age children and adolescents and every phase brings its own set of challenges for a married couple's sex life. By keeping date nights consistent and going on trips for just the two of you, without the kids, helps to keep your love life alive and well. The children are going to affect your times of sex and intimacy and if couples aren't careful, it can lead to increasing marital dissatisfaction.

Sexual Dysfunctions

It's not a comfortable topic for men to discuss, and most men will not admit to sexual dysfunctions and performance difficulties, which happen quite frequently. Some of the more common ones are premature ejaculation or the inability to form an erection. Men are resistant to getting help when these issues arise due to pride, ego, and the belief they can fix it on their own. These are conditions that have real medical solutions that can improve the sexual encounter for both you and your wife. If these are some of the problems you are facing, then you may want to consider The Boston Medical Group, with offices throughout the United States.

It could also be that your wife has some sexual difficulties like the inability to become ready for sex in her vaginal area. Some women suffer from dryness that makes sex a painful experience. A quality lubricant can help this issue, but there may be some medical concerns as well. When a woman has problems with her blood pressure, blood sugar, iron levels, this can affect her desire for sex and ability to perform. You should suggest that she consider consulting with her primary care physician.

Lastly, there are a variety of therapists who specialize in sex counseling that you and your wife may want to consider scheduling an appointment to address any problems. Choose one that shares your particular faith or value system, so that the treatment options match what you believe to be sexually moral.

Shooting Under Par

1. **Open Mind**: Sexual needs and desires change over time for both you and your wife. Being attuned with those changes over the course of your marriage will strengthen your love life.

2. **Romance**: Make it happen. Romance is desired by your wife more often than she desires the act of sexual intercourse. Enhancing your ability to be consistently romantic towards your wife deepens the bonds of intimacy.

3. **Stress-Free**: Never pressure your wife to perform a sexual act that she feels uncomfortable doing. The marriage bed is undefiled because what is done there is by two people who have committed their life to each other. The moment we pressure our spouse to do something they find immoral or degrading, is the moment we defile the marriage bed.

4. **Foreplay**: As you can imagine, foreplay looks different for everyone. For some it may mean lots of physical touch, while for others they want to be held and made to feel valued and loved. Reconciling how we want foreplay and how our wife receives and expresses it can eliminate a lot of misunderstandings and unsatisfactory sexual experiences.

5. **Frequency**: The frequency of sex varies for each couple. Some have sex once a month while others experience it ten times a month. Comparing your frequency to other couples isn't helpful, because there are various factors that determine frequency over the course of a marriage. A recent study has concluded that couples who have sex once a week do have greater marital satisfaction than couples who only have it once a month. However, there wasn't much of a satisfaction difference between

couples who did it once a week, versus those who did it more than once a week.

6. **Help**: An excellent resource to consider reading together with your spouse is a book entitled, *Intended for Pleasure,* by Ed & Gaye Wheat. This wonderful book tastefully discusses sexual technique and sexual fulfillment.

7. **Communication**: Often problems inside of the bed are due to problems outside of the bedroom. Use the *5 Love Languages* model by Dr. Gary Chapman to discover how you and your wife demonstrate and receive love. The better you are at speaking the love language of our spouse, the greater your sexual fulfillment.

CHAPTER 10

OFF THE FIELD ISSUES

"That's a common trait among many of the most talented players who weren't selected in this year's NFL draft. Teams may like your talent, but if they don't like your character, they don't want you in their locker rooms."

- Michael David Smith

The news of professional athletes having off the field issues is unfortunately a common occurrence in American sports today. Time after time we see athletes with great talent making terrible personal life decisions that derails or delays their professional career. On the field, they are incredibly successful. They have talent and are respected by their teammates. By contrast, off the field, they may have a drug, alcohol or gambling problem. Some have been charged with domestic violence assault, battery, and even homicide. While others have multiple traffic violations and DUI's. We have also seen high-profile athletes committing adultery with several women, including prostitutes. Their personal life is in terrible shape and ruining their professional life, as an accomplished athlete and person of good character.

Unfortunately, as men we have the ability to compartmentalize our life. We have the tendency to separate our personal life from our other roles and responsibilities. Taking this one dimensional position ultimately leads to our downfall, because in reality, everything in our lives is somehow connected and interrelated. This is certainly the case as it relates to men being a *great* husband.

I've seen countless husbands who are successful at work, they truly love their wife and kids, they even go to church regularly, but they just aren't winning as husbands. It's often their personal life that is hindering them from achieving greatness as a husband. Despite the promises they made to their wives to be the husband she always wanted, somehow their character isn't developed enough to ensure that those promises are kept.

Sometimes it's ignorance. Some men just don't know how to do better in certain areas of their personal life because they haven't had any positive role models to follow. For other men, it's pride and rebellion. They know what they're supposed to be doing, but they choose not to do it. Still others are failing as husbands due to unresolved anger, frustration, resentment, and fear of vulnerability that hinders them from moving away from pride and rebellion. Finally, for some men, it can be the trauma and emotional/psychological pain they experienced in childhood, adolescence, or even in adulthood, that hindered growth in their personal life.

Personal Character

In order to succeed as a husband, we have to make a commitment to consistently strengthen our character. Character development isn't a one-time action, but a daily discipline. Our personal life flows from the abundance or lack of personal character. Who we say we are needs to line up with what we do. Consistency is important in life because our external actions should be representative of our internal disposition. When our wife believes she sees consistency in us, but finds out that our "public" life doesn't measure up with our "private" or personal life, it is perceived as deception. She feels lied to, betrayed, and tricked, which is why we experience backlash from her.

The process of forming and maintaining our character is found in the things we do, say, and think about every day. The compounding effect of consistent character development results in the power to say no temptation, to deny our tendencies to do what we know is wrong, and the strength to hold onto our principles and values when life tells us to abandon them for immediate relief. Conversely, the daily neglect of character development leaves us weak to the temptations of this world and unable to fight against our worst tendencies as men. Character development doesn't mean we'll be perfect, it just means that we'll continue to grow and mature despite our missteps.

Often our character development is formed by our personal

philosophy or the narratives that live in our heart and mind. We all have certain mottos or confessions that guide our life in both good times and bad. For some, their narrative is, "No matter what I do, things don't turn out well for me, so what's the point in doing the right things. I'm going to live for me!" Others have a different narrative which says, "I can't get back yesterday and I'm not guaranteed tomorrow, all I have is this present moment to do the very best that I can with what I have where I am."

Sometimes character development means getting counseling for our issues and struggles. If at any time you realize you personally need counseling to work through past or present issues then go get the assistance you need. The longer you wait, the more damage you will do to your wife, yourself, and everyone connected to you. Most men don't like to ask for help. We put up a shield to guard our pride, ego, sense of worth, and display an image of control, strength and superiority. Conversely, this false representation gets in the way of embracing humility and accepting truth into our lives. Think about it, men don't like to ask for directions even when they are clearly lost and confused while driving to our destination. It should therefore come as no surprise that men would not be willing to ask for assistance in their personal life because that would mean embracing vulnerability and letting go of the image of power and control.

I am not exempt from this struggle either; there was a time in my marriage that my wife and I needed the help of a marriage counselor. I obviously resisted seeing a marriage counselor because I am a marriage counselor! I firmly believed that we could solve our difficulties without the assistance of a third party. I finally realized that despite my best efforts to correct my actions and solve our marital problems, it couldn't be done without a qualified third party. I certainly understand the difficulty we have as men to get help, but in the end it often turns out to be one of our greatest decisions. If we truly want to be great husbands, we must be willing to address the personal character issues that are derailing our future success.

Personal Core Values

Most of the companies we work for have a mission statement and core values. Even professional sports teams have their own mission statement and core values. The mission statement is the overall goals of the organization while the core values describe how they are going to reach their goals. As a man, one of our mission statements is to be a great husband to our wife. So I would encourage you to create your own personal core values to live by in order for that mission statement to become a reality. These core values will provide a road map for you to follow. They will help you make decisions, give you the strength to resist the temptations of life, and handle challenges successfully. It may take some time to write out your personal core values, but once it's complete, you will quickly realize that it was worth the time and effort.

Don't make your personal core values too complicated or too difficult to remember. If you can't remember the main points, then you won't live by them. Don't be afraid of using a few lines that others have already incorporated into their daily lives. If it is written well, it will resonate with your soul so just use it so you won't be up half the night trying to write like someone else. Try to limit it to one page so you see it regularly. Read it to the point where you have it memorized. To help you get started on your own core values, I've provided mine for you to see as an example. Some of them I picked up from other people, others I created myself. Hopefully, it sparks meaningful things in you as you pursue personal and marital greatness.

Pastor Jim's Core Values as a Husband & Father

1. For Things to Change I Must Change

*This speaks to personal responsibility, no more blaming others, no more excuses for not doing well, the practice of drift and neglect are no longer an option. I have to take action to make things happen.

2. Lead by Serving

*Jesus came to serve, not to be served by others. I need to meet my wife's needs and desires. Her needs are the essentials of life while her desires are her hopes and dreams for the future. I must focus on her needs, while working to fulfill her desires. I need to be the first to sacrifice and the last to be rewarded.

3. If I Can't Do It In Front Of My Wife, I Can't Do It.

*This speaks to sexual integrity, moral integrity, being honest and truthful. It helps to avoid saying or doing things that would cause conflict and pain in my wife's life and my life as well.

4. Look Well Into Every Matter

*Proverbs says the naïve believe everything but the wise look well into every matter. It's my job to look well into every matter from family, friends, finances, and opportunities. I can't take someone else's word for it, I must do my own investigation to come to my own conclusions.

5. Fear Does Not Get a Vote

*Fear will not dictate what we do or don't do. I will not allow fear to determine what we will or will not explore. Fear will not be allowed to influence or vote on any decisions. Being fearful leads to stupidity and desperate actions.

Power of Connections

According to therapist Erik Kispert, every man needs three different men in his life. The first is the banker. He's the guy who you can tell all your fears, concerns, secret sins, and he still loves you and doesn't look at you any differently. The second guy is the accountant. He is your accountability guy for your dreams, goals, and aspirations, as well as your struggles and addictions. The third guy is the director. He will help you understand your life situations (good and bad) and he can give you sound direction on how to move forward so that you'll be a success. A common question in response to hearing this advice is "can't one guy be all three of those roles?" Certainly, one person can fill all three for you, but you may face some challenges putting everything on one person. The most obvious is if the person is no longer in your life, then you've lost all three of them. A much better answer to the question is that every man should strive to have three different men fulfill these functions because it forces men to have multiple strong connections. Our lives will be richer if we can develop our male friendships to the point where we have three other men in our life with such a degree of closeness and connection.

Not only do you need the three men mentioned above, but we also need to have male friendships in our lives that will encourage and strengthen our commitment to being great men. If any of your friendships hinder you from becoming a great husband, then those friendships need to end. I'm sure you have heard it said before, "Show me your five closest friends and I'll show you where you'll be in the next ten years." Our friendships and relationships with other men or the lack thereof, greatly impacts our personal life and in turn our ability to be a great husband. It is of utmost importance to be a man of integrity and character by consistently living within your values, beliefs, and standards. Your male connections and friendships are often the determining factor in maintaining that reality.

Power of Focus

As we work on ourselves to clean up any "off the field issues," we must realize the power of focus is vitally important. In order to maximize your efforts of change and success, develop a laser-like focus on what God has asked you to do and work with what He placed in your hand. Sometimes we need to shut off the outside world in the sense that we aren't distracted by people or situations that will rob us of taking charge of our own life. We can't get distracted by comparing ourselves to men who are further along than us because we'll only get discouraged. Nor should we get distracted by comparing ourselves to men who aren't as far along as we are, because then we'll get complacent.

We also can't allow sports, politics, outside interests or hobbies distract us in our pursuit for personal growth, economic independence, and excellent family relations. There is nothing wrong with sports, politics, or hobbies, but men have the tendency to use these things (and others) to escape or ignore the reality of their lives. Sometimes we need to change our daily habits to remove the distractions and improve our rate of success. We might need to turn off the TV a few days a week. Missing SportsCenter every now and then, won't kill us. Turn off the computer and take a break from the internet and social media will also be helpful. Once we turn away from these things for a short time, it will give us the opportunity to create a solid routine that will put us on a path of success and greatness. We may need to do more. Read the Bible more. Pray more. Journal more. As you strive to capitalize on the power of focus, filter everything through the lens of, "If it robs or distracts me from taking charge of my life and pursuing greatness as a husband, in all areas of my life, then I'm not going to give it any of my focus."

Scoring Points

1. **Owning Up**: Take personal responsibility for all aspects of your life and never justify your bad behavior by highlighting the bad behavior of others.

2. **Smart Choices**: Choose your commitments wisely. Every commitment we make will bring a sense of loss because when we commit to one thing, it means we won't be able to commit to other things. If we can process the loss correctly, we'll keep to our commitments.

3. **Word Smart**: Say what you mean and mean what you say. Your wife shouldn't have to figure out if you're serious or joking. She shouldn't have to guess the state of your mind and heart. Furthermore, most wives would rather their husbands not use profanity. If she has said this to you, then honor that request.

4. **Student-Minded**: Look for ways to continue growing spiritually, relationally, emotionally, and psychologically; always remain teachable. The moment we think we've learned it all, is the moment we stop learning and therefore stop growing.

5. **Temple–wise**: Avoid destructive behavior: pornography, alcohol, drugs, cigarettes, gambling, womanizing, and anything that decreases living a long and productive

life. Your body is a temple.[13]

6. **Social Media**: Avoid doing anything on Facebook, Instagram, Twitter (or any other social networking site) that would cause your wife to question your character, or integrity.

7. **Commitment**: Never allow your words or actions with other women to cause you to cross the line over into adultery. Remain faithful to your wife in every way and in every situation.

8. **Follow through**: Stay true to the time you told your wife you'd be home from work or a personal outing. If the time you originally stated changes, show consideration and give her a call.

9. **Protector**: In every situation, make sure your wife knows you have her best interest at heart. She needs to feel protected and safe and views you as the protector of the family.

10. **Emotional Balance**: Realize that if we have unchecked, unresolved negative emotions, it leads to unintended consequences for ourselves and our marriage. These unintended consequences leads to more negative emotions and subsequently unacceptable behaviors that will significantly damage our marital relationship.

CHAPTER 11

Get Off the Bench

*"If a player's not doing the things he should, put him
on the bench. He'll come around."*

-John Wooden

When athletes are unable to execute the plays called by the
coach or another teammate, over a period of time they
soon find themselves sitting on the bench. They remain on the
team, but not on the field, because they can't be trusted to perform and produce. When men are unable or worse unwilling
to run the plays necessary to be a great husband, it results in
their wife experiencing fear, loss of trust, sadness, pain, frustration, anger, loneliness, isolation, and rejection. This in turn,
leads to the husband sitting on the proverbial "martial" bench
because when a wife experiences these unfavorable emotions,
over a period of time, she will often become more independent
out of survival, rather than dependent on her husband. She

will make sure life continues to happen at home and with the kids, but she stops calling plays for her husband. This creates at home tension, stress, periods of silence, short or curt answers. Eventually, anger settles within both of them leading to further isolation and individual action rather than teamwork. At bedtime, many husbands find themselves still on the team, but not in the game. Sitting on the bench staring at your wife who is sound asleep with her back to you, can be very burdensome.

First Steps

If your marriage is to survive in these challenging moments and get to a place of thriving, you have to work hard to get off the bench and back into the flow of the game. You can in fact get back on the marital playing field with our wife and work as teammates that trust and rely on each other. In every sport, players get off of the bench often by producing in practice first. If they get off the bench unexpectedly during a game, then it means that a starting player just got hurt and the team is in crisis mode. You don't want your relationship with your wife to get to crisis mode to get you off the bench. Start proving you're trustworthy and responsible on the practice field now with these four warmup points:

(1) You must be willing to apologize and say sorry for your actions and/or inactions that lead you to sitting on the bench.

(2) Your present and future actions must align with the apology that was offered to your wife. An apology without changed behaviors and attitudes is no apology at

all.

(3) You have to understand that your past behavior is the best predictor of future behavior. If you have a history of saying one thing, but doing another, your words of remorse mean nothing to your wife. Only your present and future actions, words, and attitudes will be able to speak for you in this instance.

(4) You must not make the mistake of thinking that once you say you're sorry, that the relationship with your wife will instantly go back to the way it was before the transgression occurred. The length of time it takes your wife to forgive you and to get you off the bench depends on your ability to execute the right plays at the right time and in the right way. Give her adequate space and time to forgive. We also must realize that the depth of pain we may have caused also affects the length of time that is needed for restoration in the relationship and for her to trust you again.

Proving You Belong On The Field

If you understand, embrace, and implement the four points mentioned earlier, then you're ready to ease your way back into the flow of the game with your wife. I've created a list of actions that have helped others and it may help you. This is certainly not an exhaustive list, and if none of them fit your situation, hopefully they will spark the creativity needed to help you get off the bench.

(1) Flowers are a timeless classic, so buy her favorite flowers

and have them delivered.

(2) They say that "Diamonds are a girl's best friend," so if you have the financial means to purchase a pair of diamond earrings or necklace, then go ahead and do it.

(3) In your own handwriting, compose a love letter for your wife. Profess your love for her, your sincere apology, how much you appreciate her, and how you always want to be married to such a wonderful woman. You should close the letter by painting a picture of the future you'll have together. I can't express the importance of the handwritten part of the exercise. You may have poor penmanship, but she'll love and appreciate it all the more if you write it out as opposed to sending an email or printing one out.

(4) Purchase a gift card to her favorite store. The amount isn't as important as the fact that you got the gift card because it shows you know what she likes and that you were thinking of her.

(5) Cancel a personal leisure activity you had planned, so that you can spend time with her doing something that she enjoys.

(6) Surprise her one evening and have dinner prepared before she comes home from work one day.

(7) Take the initiative and set up the marriage counseling sessions she has been asking you to do, but you have been procrastinating about it for some time.

(8) When she comes home from a long hard day at work, draw a warm bubble bath for her to relax and enjoy.

Make sure there is soft music playing, the lights are dimmed and candles are lit. While she is resting in the tub, take care of dinner and/or the kids, so that after her bath, she can continue to relax for the evening.

(9) Send some "just thinking of you" emails, text messages, or social media posts to her. These can be done just once or perhaps throughout the day depending on what is needed to make things right. I would caution against multiple social media posts. One post is fine, but if you want to do multiple postings, it would be better to do it through emails or text messages that only the two of you can see.

(10) Discover, learn, and speak her love language regularly. Author Dr. Gary Chapman has written a book entitled, *The 5 Love Languages*, where he states that there are 5 different love languages a person has: i) Acts of service, ii) Words of affirmation, iii) Physical touch, iv) Receiving gifts, and v) Quality time. Getting off the bench will require you to speak your wife's love language.

The willingness to do these things, and others that you create, will help to restore your relationship, get you off the bench and back in the game. It's never easy to ask for forgiveness or make amends for past wrongs, but it is always the right thing to do. Furthermore, as long as you are still married and trying to make things work in your relationship, it's never too late to start doing what's right.

Conflict Resolution & Communication Success

The times when we fight or argue with our wives can be filled with pitfalls and landmines. When emotions are high, stress has settled in and when both parties feel they're right is a dangerous time for the relationship. In these moments, it is so easy to make mistakes and cause things to get worse rather than improve. If you find yourself in this difficult situation, it's good to remember the Five R's: Right Time, Right Speech, Right Attitude, Right Response, Right Repair Attempt.

Right Time

Timing is truly important. Some circumstances require us to address a situation immediately. Other times, it may actually be more healthy and appropriate to address the issue at a later date. When we give ourselves time before discussing something with our wife it allows both parties the chance to get their raw emotion and the accompanying words out of our system before they say something they may regret. It's a good idea to have the conversation with yourself to get your initial thoughts and feelings out. So consider the moments when you need a moment before having that difficult conversation. When you know what you want and need to say, you must determine when is the right time to have this conversation. A good time for you, may not be the best time for her. Make sure you feel out her mood, energy level, and stress level from the day, to know it's the Right Time.

Right Speech

We alluded to this in the right time section. You'll need to know the right words to use to express your thoughts. Words are powerful, they are seeds that we plant into the heart and mind of our wife. We must choose our speech carefully and constructively. I often teach married couples to implement "I" statements. You start with "I" then state your feeling(s) along with a fact to convey your thoughts and emotions. If the sentence starts with "you" and offers opinions it puts people on the defensive and unable to truly hear what you wanted conveyed. The Right Speech is vital to this equation.

Right Attitude

You can select the right time, use the right words, but if you have the wrong attitude during the conversation you won't get your desired results of reconciliation. Our attitudes are critically important in these moments. Your attitude can change the atmosphere in your home. Check your attitude at the door and make sure it conveys honesty, humility, along with genuine love, care and concern for her and the relationship. If your attitude stinks of arrogance, pride, condemnation, and self-righteousness, things will spiral downhill quickly.

Right Response

So after you've selected the right time, the right speech, and the right attitude and begun the conversation, she'll be amenable to listen to what is being said. Be ready and prepared for her to you, along with all of the things she's been thinking about and wanting to say. It's in this moment you need the Right Response to her. Your responses to her demonstrate you truly hear, understand, and validate her experience and feelings. I've witnessed men get the first three R's correct, but then blow it on the fourth R. Their response to her questions were defensive, or they made excuses for their actions/inactions. Worse off, many men tried to convince their wives that they shouldn't feel a particular way. Keep in mind that we need the Right Response to get our desired results of reconciliation, renewal, or reconnection with our wives.

Right Repair Attempts

The concept of Repair Attempts comes from the work done by Dr. John Gottman in his book, *The 7 Principles for Making Marriage Work*. He says that repair attempts are things that couples say or do when they realize their communication is escalating into a conflict. It could be an inside joke, a phrase that has special meaning to them, or a funny face. It's something that both the husband and wife agree upon ahead of time so that when the conversation is getting heated and climbing up the mountain of conflict, it reminds both of them to take a step back. This gives them a chance to compose themselves so that their connection is maintained and arguments without resolution are avoided. We often will climb the mountain of conflict until we reach the pinnacle and nothing is resolved and both climb back down the mountain with hurt feelings, resentment and frustration. If this has been a common occurrence for you and your wife, then perhaps your repair attempt could be, "let's not climb the mountain." Making a conscious effort to repair conversations the moments they go wrong, ensures you will have a greater resolution, more frequent reconciliation, and remain connected to each other.

Communication Time-Out

In any sport, the coach or player calls a time out to regroup, get out of a jam, or to take their opponent out of rhythm. Time-outs are critical and it is a time for the players to really focus. For this reason, to further emphasize the five R's to resolve conflict and have communication success, I have called a thirty second time-out. We can't have three out of the five R's or two out of the five, and think the conversation will lead to reconnection. The great thing about the five R's is that they are all totally under our control. We aren't dependent on our wives to ensure the five R's work correctly. If you successfully implement the five R's and the outcome isn't positive, you can walk away from that conversation knowing you did what you could. More than likely, there may be something internally your wife has to work through. It could be that you've been screwing up the playbook for some time and she has over the months or years pent up anger and frustration. Now that you're willing to be open and talk, she feels free enough to share what she had been holding onto inside, but didn't think it was safe enough to discuss with you. We must learn to give the process time to work things out so that your road to being a great husband can get the green light.

FOURTH QUARTER

CHAPTER 12

A Word to the Wives

"Next to every great man is an even greater woman."

-Jim Hart

Ladies, all of these plays may be applicable for you and your husband, but some have more meaning and significance to you. It is in your best interest as a wife to tell your husband which plays are the most meaningful. This allows him to prioritize those plays above the others to give them special attention in his life. The influence and power of a loving and attentive wife is profound in the development and growth of a man as a husband. Ralph Waldo Emerson said it best, "A man's wife has more power over him than the State has."

I'm sure that you've heard that behind every great man is a great woman. I disagree with that statement as I believe that next to every great man is an even greater woman. My own experience and the experience of so many other men bear this testimony. I wouldn't be the man or husband I am today if it weren't for my wife. The love and care she demonstrates to me along with the correction and education she gives me, helped to shape and refine me into the husband I am today. Occasionally she'll jokingly say that she won't ever leave me because she's invested too much into me and worked too hard to get me right where she wants me. She has stated that she wouldn't want to start over with anyone else. I know it might sound as though I saying that men ought to be henpecked. That couldn't be further from the truth. The lesson I am trying to convey here is that wives have the potential to make a powerful, positive impact on the lives of their husbands. Wives need to recognize and appropriately use that power and influence. Husbands on the other hand, need to be humble and mature enough to listen and follow the advice and guidance his wife provides.

Many wives have been waiting for their husbands to read their minds. These wives have been frustrated because their husband hasn't read their mind yet about things that mean the most to them. Although it is his responsibility to take the spiritual leadership in the home, know that it doesn't come with a divine power to read people's minds. Other times, wives don't want mind readers, they just complain that their husband should know some of these things by now. I will certainly admit that sometimes we men aren't paying attention to what you have been asking for very directly or indirectly. This causes us to miss important things in your life that we really should have known.

There are however, other moments when we can't be blamed

for ignorance due to the lack of attention we've given to our wives. Some things we genuinely don't know and couldn't have known because you have not told us. More times than I like to remember, in counseling sessions, I've asked the wife if she ever told her husband what she really wanted or was concerned about or had deep fears over. Her answer is often, "No, because I didn't think he would listen to me!" He may have not been listening to you in the past, but you are both now reading this book and he is in a better place to hear you now. So go ahead and be as clear and honest as possible with your husband in order for him to become *great*. If you keep the perspective that he will never listen to you, you are actually keeping him imprisoned to your past experiences and therefore he can never be freed to live out his fullest potential.

Unfortunately, your husband isn't perfect and as such he will at one time or another after reading this book fail to run some of these plays. He is going to drop the ball...strike out... and miss the shot. When he fails, don't hammer him to the point where he despises the playbook. The strategies are here to help improve the relationship, so when there are broken plays, focus on what is happening in the relationship. If you use these strategies as a stick to bring obedience from your husband and not as a stone to build your life together, then you'll be missing the power and purpose of these secrets in the first place. It's up to you. How you respond to him when he does and doesn't abide by these strategies will significantly determine whether he will continue to adhere to them in the future.

Another important point is that you need to recognize that

your husband is not you! What I mean is that your husband isn't going to do things exactly the way you do them nor sometimes the way you ask him to do them. This issue can be most easily observed when it comes to household responsibilities. He may not make the bed the way you make the bed. He may not fold the clothes the way you fold the clothes. He many not iron the way you iron. He may not clean the bathroom the way you clean the bathroom. He may not go grocery shopping the way you go shopping. The possible examples of performing certain tasks are endless. The point is, don't get on your husband if he doesn't do the household chores exactly like you do them. He'll probably never do it exactly the way you do it because he's not you! If you harp on him about how he doesn't do it like you do it he will be less likely to do the chore at all in the future. You shouldn't be concerned about replication of the task, but rather be appreciative of the assistance he is offering and make constructive suggestions on how he can improve. This suggestion isn't to make him more like you, but to help him be the best he can be at whatever task he is endeavoring to accomplish.

For some of you, your husband has been violating these plays for some time which has caused a lot of pain. I would encourage you to be willing to forgive him. Allow him the time and space to live out these new plays with you. It will take him some time before he can internalize and actually live them out. Yet if you continue to see effort on his part, and progression towards growth, maturity, and greatness, this will give you the hope you need to trust him again. If however, he doesn't improve and refuses to internalize and implement these strategies, then you'll have some difficult decisions moving forward. Before you make any final decision, I strongly suggest you speak with a trusted counselor who can offer you insight and perspective to your situation.

I would encourage you that you have power when it comes to extending forgiveness. As husbands, it is our responsibility to ask for forgiveness when we ignore and screw up these plays. As wives, it is your responsibility to extend that forgiveness when asked for it. I'm not saying you should be a doormat with no boundaries. I'm also not saying to blindly disregard inappropriate, destructive, or dysfunctional thoughts and/or actions by your husband. What I am saying is that when your husband genuinely asks for forgiveness and there is changed behavior on his part, you should forgive him. If you don't forgive, it is only going to cause you more harm and further divide the two of you. If you are struggling in the areas of forgiveness, I strongly recommend R.T. Kendal's book, *Total Forgiveness*. In it, he explains what total forgiveness is and what it is not and I believe it will be beneficial to you.

My hope and prayer is that you won't take a jaded view of his actions in the future as he tries to implement these strategies. Keep an open heart and mind that change can happen, and when it does, acknowledge the improvement you see demonstrated in your husband. If you do this, your marital life will get better because he will feel appreciated and valued as a man which motivates him to continue doing the right thing.

Others of you have husbands who are doing a good job but

you know they can do a better job to become a *great* husband. Your husband will probably have an easier time implementing these strategies than the husband who hasn't been following many of them. Remember, don't use the plays as a stick, but rather as a stone to continue to build your life together. Help him to be the best he can be and not a carbon copy of you. Even good husbands will become resistant to correction or suggestions for improvement if they think their wives aren't appreciative of their efforts. Your husband will feed off of your actions, so make your interactions with him cause him to quote the line that Jack Nicholson used in the movie, *As Good As It Gets,* when he said to Helen Hunt, "you make me want to be a better man." If he is a better man, he can in turn be a *great* husband to you-the man you've always needed and wanted.

Top Five Needs of a Husband

Earlier in this playbook I talked about the top five needs of a wife. I provided this so that your husband could fulfill your needs and thus improve the marriage. Here, I have provided you with the top five needs of a husband, so that you in turn can meet his needs. Marriage is definitely a team effort, so I hope you find them beneficial:

1. Support

Over the years, regardless of age, race, religion, or number of years married, men have repeatedly listed "support" in their top five needs from their wives. They often mention needs like understanding and empathy. Many desire for their wives to be supportive of their career, interests, ministry activities, and supportive of the direction they believe the family should be headed. Amazingly, these husbands are saying please support me, support what I do, who I am, and where I am going. I've learned from marriage counseling, when a man doesn't feel supported it can be demoralizing, frustrating, and it further worsens the temptation to be self-centered or disengaged from his wife or family. The Bible states that a wife is a Helpmate to her husband (EN: Genesis 2:18). This title of helper is of great worth and significance. Even God is called our helper; it's the same use of the term. If a wife will support her husband both in word and deed, it will give him the strength and motivation to be the man he was created to be.

2. Sex

Statistically, if "support" was #1, then sex came in at 1A. They were so close. Husbands need and want sex regularly. It is how men are wired. It is a legitimate need that they have. Yes, it can become perverted or twisted or the husband can become selfish when it comes to sex. If that has occurred, marriage counselors don't work on fixing what is occurring in the bed, but what is happening outside of the bed. Unfortunately, when there is tension or conflict in a marriage, sex is the often the first thing that wives withhold from their husbands. There are also so many layers to a satisfied, fulfilled sexual life within a marriage that would take a lot more pages to discuss. Please embrace the truth that men honestly need sex. Furthermore, men desire intimacy as well as to have sex with their wives. If your husband genuinely loves you, just the physical act of sex is not enough for him, he wants to be intimate with you as well.

3. Respect

This probably doesn't come as a surprise. Dr. Emerson Egger-ichs wrote the classic book, *Love and Respect*, which is founded on the scripture verse that says husbands love your wives, and wives respect your husbands. Dr. Eggerichs states that when arguments or problems occur in a marriage, men most likely feel disrespected or a lack of respect from their wives. A key for wives having a happy home is to respect her husband. You will not always agree with his decisions or like some of his actions, but you can always respect him. Disrespect by a wife hardens a husband's heart, causing him to draw away from you. You'll never improve your husband or your marriage with disrespect. However, respect can soften any hardened heart and open his mind to what you want or need in the marriage.

4. Love

Husbands want to be loved, cared for, and desire to have a loving wife. Wives often do a good job at loving their husbands, but the disconnect comes from the love language she is using. Dr. Gary Chapman's book, *The 5 Love Languages*, states that we speak a certain love language and often the language we speak is the language we want spoken to us. As I mentioned earlier, *The 5 Love Languages* are: Words of Affirmation, Quality Time, Gifts, Physical Touch, and Acts of Service. I encourage you to discover your husband's love language and begin speaking it regularly. Although he may not verbalize it, he longs for you to love him. Speaking his love language shows him that at a deep level, you understand him and that he is worthy of your love.

5. Friendship

I thought that trust or appreciation would round out the top five. Instead, it was friendship. Many husbands use phrases like having fun together, quality time, companionship, partnership, and quality time with my wife. Men often build relationships and connections through activity. So it makes sense that husbands want to spend time doing fun things with their wives to build the relationship. I know that many wives are trying to get their husbands to connect with other men and do activities together, but don't lose sight of the fact that your husband probably wants to spend time doing fun activities with you as well. Your husband wants to value your friendship and see it grow throughout the years. A healthy friendship is one of the key ingredients to having a lasting marriage.

Top Five Areas of Husbands Distrust

Since I included this playbook the top five areas that wives struggle trusting their husbands, I wanted to provide you with the same information to give you a glimpse into some of the areas that husbands often don't trust their wives.

1. Money

When husbands don't trust their wives with money, it is usually due to the fact that he is the saver and she is the spender. I have heard husbands say in counseling sessions, "I don't trust her to stick to the budget, every time I turn around she is spending more money." Most times he knows she isn't going to put the family in financial jeopardy, but deep within his heart he worries if they will live like this the rest of their lives. Money is often one of the main arguments with married couples. I don't know your financial situation, so I would ask you to just take a personal inventory of how you are either contributing to increasing this distrust or eliminating it from his list of concerns.

2. Vulnerabilities/Weaknesses

Husbands are often unwilling to share their vulnerabilities and weaknesses with their wives. They don't trust that she will understand or be supportive. They also don't trust that their wives will forgive them if they reveal a moment of weakness. I'm not talking about an affair, but more like he is really struggling to not cheat on his job to advance his career. He wants to be able to confide in you, but he struggles with trust, regardless if you have demonstrated to be trustworthy in the past. It can be of an issue of male pride and ego, of not wanting to look weak or not in control. It's also a fear that you will never forget the vulnerability or will hold his weak moments over his head into the future. You want to create a relationship with your husband where he can trust you in these important areas.

3. Let Go of the Past

This is often connected with the vulnerabilities and weaknesses. Husbands aren't sure if their wives will let go of their past mistakes, or when they yielded to a weakness or vulnerability. If a husband thinks his wife won't let go of it and will constantly remind him of the past, he will not open up to her. Just like with money, I would ask you to take a personal inventory of the atmosphere you have created with your husband in this regard. Are you holding on to his past mistakes today when he has asked for forgiveness and changed directions?

4. Support His Career

Husbands in counseling sessions have told me that they don't trust that their wives support their career. Of course, you want him to work, you like the paycheck, but whenever he has to do something extra that takes time away from the family, you give him "the business" about it. Many husbands interpret this as, *my wife doesn't support my career.* A man will derive a lot of satisfaction from his work and he wants to share this experience with you. If he feels you don't support his career, he will slowly remove you from this area of his life, which ultimately is something I know you don't want to occur.

5. Sex

Husbands have told me that they don't trust that their wife

will understand and hear their desire for variety in sex and intimacy. They were not asking for anything inappropriate or immoral, but wanted to try a new position or bring in items to enhance the sexual experience. Husbands often don't trust that their wives would see it as a way to enhance their lovemaking, and worse see it as perverted. Husbands have mentioned that their wives have immediately dismissed or ignored their requests for variety, so they just stopped asking. When your husband is coming from a place of love and not lust with his sexual requests, I would encourage you to listen to him and thoughtfully consider the genuineness of where it is coming from, rather than dismissing something important to him.

Husband Appreciation Day: April 19th Every Year

It Takes Two

I know you will agree that your husband is not perfect—neither are you. If you haven't been doing a good or great job as a wife, then it's time for you to be open for change and work on those areas you struggle with as well. Your husband is reading this book as well and trying to improve in his role, even though you haven't been your best. This should encourage you and give you hope because it means one of two things: he loves you regardless of the current state of the marriage and/or he takes the vows he made to you seriously and is committed to improving as a husband. Allow these truths to encourage your heart to take the necessary steps to improve yourself as a person and as a wife.

Your improvement and growth will only motivate him that much more to continue improving which will allow his growth trajectory to soar. If you choose to remain as you have been, it may demoralize your husband's efforts to improve which ultimately leads to a loveless, lifeless marriage that will probably end in divorce. On the other hand, your husband may be more determined to focus on his personal development knowing that he cannot control you, nor make you do anything you don't want to do. My hope is that you'll take inventory of how you've been as a wife and then take the necessary steps to improve. I encourage you to be his indispensable companion. This kind of companion is not a critic, competitor, nor a complainer. Criticism won't propel him forward, it only makes him less willing to change. Competitiveness will cause a situation where someone wins and the other loses. Complaining may make him initially change, but eventually he'll stop listening to you.

Now is the time to step up your game as well. Your husband is committed to being *great* and being the best that he can be. He is making changes and so should you. I trust that you know what your issues and idiosyncrasies are. Therefore, I advise you not to wait until April 19th to demonstrate your appreciation to your husband. Make a conscious effort to show love, support and constant teamwork for your husband's efforts every day of the year.

CHAPTER 13

POST GAME SUMMARY

A FINAL WORD FROM COACH HART

"Each person holds so much power within themselves that needs to be let out. Sometimes they just need a little nudge, a little direction, a little support, a little coaching, and the greatest things can happen."

-Pete Carroll

In every sport, there is a coach to teach, motivate, and inspire the players. Players can't truly be successful without great coaching. Even the greatest professional athletes, such as Tiger Woods, Michael Jordan, Derek Jeter, Peyton Manning, all of them had great coaches. A coach is able to step back, watch the athlete perform, and can see things that the player cannot. The players often know when something is wrong, but can't always see how best to fix it. This is where the coach takes center stage.

There was a time when my golf swing was so poor that I could no longer hit the ball straight. I'm not a scratch golfer, but for the most part, I could hit the ball and in doing so enjoy a round with my friends. At one time, I could no longer hit the ball where it needed to go, and worse, I couldn't figure out what I was doing wrong. It got so bad, that I considered quitting the game of golf altogether, because it wasn't fun anymore. It was incredibly frustrating to love something so much and be unable to enjoy it. I decided to take a one-hour golf lesson hoping that the pro could correct my swing. I was a bit skeptical that my problems could be solved.

I met my golf instructor, Warren on the practice tee. *He didn't look like he could play golf much less teach it,* I thought to myself. "OK Jim, take a few swings and let me see what we are working with," he said. After about four shots, Warren looked at me and said, "I have good news and bad news. The good news is that I can correct your swing in 15 minutes." "What's the bad news?" I asked. "After I fix your swing, I'm not sure what we'll do for the next 45 minutes!" Warren first changed my grip, because that was the start of the problem. He then changed my stance so that I placed the ball closer to my left foot (I swing right-handed). Lastly, he slightly tweaked my take away and he said everything else is fine. Once I understood what he asked me to do I stepped up to the ball for my first swing with these new corrections. The first swing I hit the ball straight for 170 years. The second swing, straight and even further. The third time I had the same result. I looked up at Warren and said, "you're a genius!" He smiled and replied, "I simply saw what was wrong and led you in the direction to fix it."

Warren only made a few minor changes that made a major difference. That experience with Warren reminded me of my role as a Pastor and Marriage Counselor. Husbands and wives come in for counseling because they know something is wrong, but they don't necessarily know how to fix it. They love each other, but they aren't able to enjoy each other because of the problems and challenges they face. Sometimes the problems have gotten so bad they have contemplated divorce. At times, they come into the sessions skeptical that things can't be improved. My hope is that by reading this book, I have provided enough coaching that identified the areas where improvement can be made and lead you through the common examples that you apply to help solve the issues that have interfered with your success as a husband.

Hopefully, I've helped you get a better grip on our role and responsibility as a husband. Knowing not only what we're supposed to do as husbands, but also how to do it, can encourage and inspire us to be great. I hope that I helped to change your stance towards your wife, so that you can be closer to her and thereby love, care, protect and cherish her. Just like my take away where my golf swing had to be tweaked, I hope you take away these plays the necessary empowerment to fulfill all the dreams and aspirations you've had about your wife and marriage since the day of your wedding.

Regardless of where you find yourself today, you can truly become a *great* husband. I count it a privilege to be a small part of the journey towards success that you're going to enjoy in the days ahead. If in the future, your marital "golf swing" as a husband needs a little tweaking, don't hesitate to go get another lesson. There are plenty of qualified marriage counselors in your local area that are more than equipped to coach you.

Thank you for taking the time to read this book. It has been my great honor and pleasure to be your coach as you've read through the pages. I pray that every challenge you are facing will be addressed, every situation resolved, every heartache healed, every wound restored, and every desire that you and your wife have as a couple, be fulfilled for *Team Family*.

I look forward to hearing from you. Feel free to contact me and share how this book has helped you become a *great* husband. Log on to thegreathusbandsplaybook.com.

About the Author

Jim Hart is the Pastor of Pastoral Care and Counseling and Director of Church Development at the Abundant Life Family Worship Church where Bishop George Searight is the Senior Pastor. He has been an active member of Abundant Life since June of 1997. He facilitates the counseling ministry at the church, oversees the various ministries, functions as the church's community liaison, and is the church's Golf Tournament Co-Chairman.

Jim received a Master's in Social Work from Rutgers University and is a Licensed Social Worker in the state of NJ. He is also working on his second Master's Degree from the New Brunswick Theological Seminary matriculating through their Master's in Theological Studies program.

Jim is also an Adjunct Professor for the Graduate School of Social Work at Rutgers University where he teaches three courses: Psychopathology, Spirituality in Social Work, and Human Behavior and the Social Environment.

After 12 years of counseling and life coaching at the church and various organizations, Jim formed The Hart Company in 2012. Through his company, Jim offers counseling, coaching, workshops, and seminars to married and engaged couples. He also provides workshops and seminars in the areas of family, leadership, and diversity for churches and businesses. His popular *Coaching Calls for Married Couples* have blessed more than 100 couples.

Jim is married to his wife Yetunde and they have three children, Samuel, Daniel, and Gabriel. For Jim, being a husband and father is his greatest joy and responsibility.

RESOURCES

Throughout this book I mentioned a few resources that can assist you and your wife in various areas:

Christian Counseling Services

The American Association of Christian Counselors can be found at http://www.aacc.net. Once there, click on the tab "Find a Counselor" and follow the prompts to locate one in your local area. They also have several resources addressing a variety of concerns.

New Life Live can be found at http://www.newlife.com. Once there, click on the tab "Counseling Network" to locate a therapist in your area. They also have several resources addressing a variety of concerns.

Mental Health

The National Alliance on Mental Illness can be found at http://www.nami.org. They also provide assistance to those struggling with a mental illness as well as offer support to family members with loved ones diagnosed with a mental illness.

Sexual Health

The Boston Medical Group can be found at http://www.bostonmedicalgroup.com. They help men who are experiencing sexual dysfunctions and difficulties.

Financial

Dave Ramsey can be found at http://www.daveramsey.com. His company offers a variety of products to improve your finances, from debt elimination, saving, and investing. You will also find information on his Financial Peace University.

ENDNOTES

1   Ephesians 5:22-24

2   Matthew 20:26

3   Mathew 20:16

4   Genesis 3:1-12

5   1 Corinthians 7:33

6   Proverbs 21:9

7   1 Peter 4:8

8   1 Corinthians 7:28

9   Proverbs 13:22

10 James 1:22-23

11 James 2:14-26

12 Deuteronomy 32:30

13 1 Corinthians 6:19

FOR MORE INFORMATION OR FOR BOOKINGS LOG ON TO:

Thegreathusbandsplaybook.com

Made in the USA
Middletown, DE
13 February 2016